THE MAP OF MY
DEAD PILOTS

THE MAP OF MY
DEAD PILOTS

THE DANGEROUS GAME OF FLYING IN ALASKA

COLLEEN MONDOR

LYONS PRESS
Guilford, Connecticut
An imprint of Globe Pequot Press

Lyons Press is an imprint of Globe Pequot Press.

Project editor: David Legere
Text design: Sheryl P. Kober
Layout: Kirsten Livingston

Map background licensed by Shutterstock.com

"On the Other Side of the Mountains" first appeared in a slightly different form in the *Anchorage Press,* Anchorage, Alaska; "Mercy Flight" first appeared in a slightly different form in the online magazine *Storyglossia;* "Our Missing Airman" first appeared in a slightly different form in the online magazine *Identity Theory;* and "The Truth about Flying" first appeared in a slightly different form in the literary journal *ZYZZYVA,* San Francisco, California.

ISBN 978-0-7627-8686-2

Printed in the United States of America

10 9 8 7 6 5 4 3 2 1

The Library of Congress has previously catalogued an earlier (hardcover) edition as follows:

Mondor, Colleen Catherine.
  The map of my dead pilots : the dangerous game of flying in Alaska / Colleen Mondor.
    p. cm.
  ISBN 978-0-7627-7361-9
  1. Bush pilots—Alaska—Biography. 2. Bush pilots—Alaska—Death. 3. Bush pilots—Alaska—Psychology. 4. Aircraft accidents—Alaska. 5. Aircraft accidents—Human factors—Alaska. 6. Risk-taking (Psychology)—Alaska. 7. Bush flying—Alaska. 8. Aeronautics, Commercial—Social aspects—Alaska. 9. Aeronautics, Commercial—Alaska—Psychological aspects. 10. Alaska—Biography. I. Title.
  TL539.M58 2012
  387.7092'2798—dc23

                                                        2011033005

For everyone at the Company, but especially
Dave, Chris, Andy, and Ward
And also, in loving memory,
Robert R. Mondor (1939–1999)

Contents

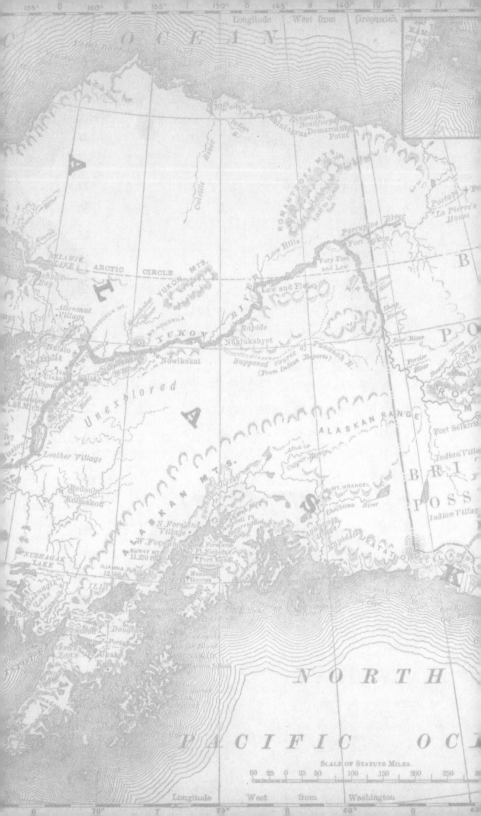

Preface

I was initially quite reticent to publish this book as a memoir, preferring the more forgiving fiction route as a way to keep the stories true but the names and places less factual. I was persuaded to refocus my narrative and bring it back to the way it was—the way all of us who were part of the Company knew it to be true, but with the caveat that the identities of the people I worked with could still be protected. None of them, after all, ever expected to have their exploits shared with the world. So rest assured that all of these flights, all the accidents, the crashes, and the near misses did take place as described in these pages (curious readers can in fact find a list of the actual NTSB accident reports at my website), but the names of the participants have been changed because I sincerely believe that was the right thing to do. There are a few exceptions to this rule: the historic names remain as listed (Ben Eielson, Russ Merrill, etc.), and I did have a dearly missed friend named John Hitz who died impossibly young in a snow machine crash in Fairbanks. Also, my friend Jen Nelson did indeed fly both a dead frozen seal and a "head in a box." She will, I'm sure, be amused to have readers know just how unglamorous Alaska flying can be.

The time frame I worked at the Company remains unchanged (1993–1997) and the period after I left, while working on my graduate thesis at the University of Alaska Fairbanks on the causes of pilot error accidents among commercial pilots in the state, is exactly as I present it here. I did however take some experiences that happened to multiple pilots I worked with over the years at the Company (dozens) and ascribe them to the pilots I name in this narrative. It simply became too complicated to keep straight all the names when sharing only a single brief incident for many of them (such as being chased around an airplane by a knife-wielding passenger), so pilots I named Tony, Sam, Scott, Frank, Casey and Bob are sometimes combinations of more than one individual, but again everything did happen and it happened to all of us.

Someone I call Adam did crash for reasons he cannot understand even today, someone I call Ray did run out of gas over the sea ice off of Nome with a girl's high school basketball team onboard, someone I call Luke did lose his life chasing wolves on a beautiful day without a cloud in the sky, and someone I call Bryce did die in a crash with the Yukon River. I remember all of these moments; I still have the accident reports beside me, and I still talk to Adam about what went wrong on a flight where everything could have gone right.

Because *Map* deals with pilots, there is a certain amount of aviation terminology that had to be included. Whenever possible I have explained these terms in the surrounding text, but some words might still be puzzling for those unfamiliar with our industry. For example, when a pilot refers to "losing his tickets" he means the revocation or suspension of his FAA licenses which permit him to legally fly. CAVU stands for "ceiling and visibility unlimited" and thus means crystal clear flying conditions. A VOR is a type of radio navigation system for aircraft that can be used for air navigation from place to place. To land at an airport during inclement weather requires the presence of at least one of a variety of different types of instrumentation such as an Instrument Landing System (ILS), with possibly a published localizer back course approach or a Nondirectional Beacon (NDB).

The most common aviation terminology I use in the book is "VFR into IMC," which stands for operating under "visual flight rules into instrument meteorological conditions," and it is the most common cause of pilot error accidents in Alaska. It generally means "a pilot flying by reference to outside visual cues flew into low visibility conditions." In the case of VFR into IMC accidents, the flight typically ends with the pilot losing control and/or hitting terrain. VFR rules change depending on the class of airspace you are flying in, but generally in Alaska VFR pilots must be five hundred feet below, one thousand feet above, and two thousand feet horizontal from clouds, and have three miles visibility unless you are within one thousand two hundred feet of the surface. In Alaska, because of the lack of instrumentation at airfields, many airports allow VFR approaches only. Pilots will often depart under VFR with the intention to "go look and see" if the weather conditions permit them to land on a field. When encountering IMC conditions, they should turn back but some do not or become disoriented and cannot find their way out.

I continue to remember my time at the Company with great fondness, and in no small measure due to the lifelong friendships I forged there. It may not be reality television, but it was our lives at a job we were good at, and a time and place we will never forget.

Colleen Mondor
June 10, 2011

1

The Truth about Flying

Sam Beach went to Alaska seeking redemption, reflection, a rehearsal for the rest of his life. He told his family it was only for a year, maybe two, and he believed it when he said it. He believed everything about Alaska: the books, the magazines, the endless supply of cable TV shows.

Especially the TV shows.

He fell hard for the myths, even though he pretended not to. *Outside* magazine said that becoming a bush pilot was one of the fifty things you must do in your life. And because he couldn't stand the thought of one more day flight instructing for minimum wage, he read that article again and again. He read it a hundred times.

He didn't see himself as Ben Eielson, heading to Fairbanks in 1922 on his way to fame and glory as the first pilot to fly across the Arctic. By 1995 commercial flying in Alaska wasn't really about the bush anymore; it was about commuter schedules and hauling mail and building flight time to get a jet job. But he still had that same vision of Eielson's in his head: This time it would be different; this time the job wouldn't go away; this time he would make it. Sam had been in aviation long enough to know what Alaska meant; it was the place where pilots were needed, where they *mattered*. This is my chance, he told his parents, and he said it just like Eielson did so long ago, with promises to be smart and careful and come home again soon.

He said it like he believed it, and maybe then he did. Sam believed a lot of things in the beginning, and he learned to repeat those things every time his parents called, even after he realized they were lies. And he never told them Ben Eielson crashed in 1929. And of course they never thought to ask.

Some things never do change after all.

———•———

The things they had to know were endless. From their first day flying for the Company, they filled their heads with facts and figures of length and distance, knowledge of rivers and mountains, the location of a hundred landmarks, or a thousand. They learned when it was safe to drop down through the clouds, when they might continue forward, when they must turn right or left, when they absolutely had to turn back. They made sure sled dogs were tied on short leashes because one of them would jump on another and cause a fight at the worst possible time. They understood why they needed to strap down dead bodies extra tight after Frank Hamilton had one slip free on takeoff. (Frank was superstitious, although he wouldn't admit it, and the sound of that body sliding back and forth all the way in from Koyukuk sent him right to Pike's for a beer minutes after he got back to Fairbanks. His plan was to be too drunk to drive home as quickly as possible.)

No one liked flying with bodies.

They learned to respect the cold and then hate it. They became cautious or cocky, whatever worked. And in spite of themselves, they started laughing at everything, because it really was funny when they took the time to think about it. "We're just a bunch of damn bus drivers," Tony would say, "glorified bus drivers."

"Bus drivers in Mexico," said Sam, "a really lousy part of Mexico."

"Fuck that, more like bus drivers on the moon," said Frank. "No one does this kind of work anywhere else for the pay we're getting. Might as well be on the moon."

And they all nodded because he was right. Seventy years after the first bush pilots took a million crazy chances to get the job done, the Company might as well have been the moon for all that the rules applied. It was truly the ends of the earth, or even farther if you were making a living in the cockpit.

———

To combat boredom, most of them flew with reading material. There were magazines, paperback novels, the *Fairbanks Daily News-Miner,* and for the more ambitious, yesterday's copy of the *Wall Street Journal.* They packed their flight bags with flashlights and Leathermans, sunglasses and seatbelt extenders, gloves and extra batteries. Since state law allowed it and because most of them were pessimists, they also carried guns.

Tony flew with a 9-millimeter and Scott Young a .44; Frank had a .45. Bob didn't have the money to buy a gun and Casey didn't have the guts to buy one, although he always asked Frank if he could plink cans with his. No one knew what Bryce carried, but it didn't matter anymore anyway because it was taken away along with everything else when he crashed in the Yukon River one summer day in 1999.

A lot of things disappeared forever when Bryce died.

If you knew someone who had been stuck on the ground in the boonies, then you knew the gun was necessary equipment. Tony grew up in Fairbanks and had a friend hit the side of a mountain and lay out there, stuck for hours with her passenger, waiting for a rescue with two broken legs and a cargo of chips and canned goods. The thought of being circled by hungry bears was enough to make anyone put a pistol in their flight bag. Sam just looked at it as another tool—he had a ratchet set, tie wire, and a pistol. And Frank? Frank took his with him to bed at night.

But that was Frank.

They packed bag lunches and thermoses full of hot coffee. They remembered to bring knives, forks, and spoons. If they were going to Galena or Barrow or Deadhorse, where they knew there would be a microwave and a place to eat, they carried TV dinners. If it was fire season, they angled for flights into Bettles or McGrath, where they could scam a box lunch from the fire service. In the winter they ate early, before their sandwiches froze on the floor beside them.

Tony dumped a packet of Instant Breakfast into his thermos of coffee to keep him awake on the early morning cargo run, while Casey just mainlined Mountain Dew no matter when he was flying. Frank brought lunch from home; Scott did too, until his wife left him, taking his kid, his dog, his money, and every single piece of Tupperware. He started eating out of the vending machines then, and raiding the company fridge.

Because he was addicted, Bob Stevens packed cigarettes. For a little while he wore a nicotine patch, but it didn't do any good. The patch couldn't defeat all the reasons Bob needed cigarettes, couldn't bring his father back from the dead or make him a decent man once he returned. It couldn't make his mother understand that just because her childhood was crap didn't mean that everyone else's had to be too, and it couldn't make that girl, that last girl he saw in Seattle, not tell him he was lousy in bed.

The patch couldn't stop Bob's palms from sweating, his heart from racing, or his mouth from going dry when he was faced with another day of flying an overloaded airplane into questionable weather just to prove to the Bosses who didn't give a shit about him, to the other pilots who barely noticed him, or to himself, who was too crippled to care, that he, Bob Stevens, was indeed man enough. He felt like the cigarettes gave him an edge, an image; they made it all seem possible, even enjoyable. He was the Marlboro Man out there, flying at five hundred feet looking for something to see. He almost felt good with the pack resting in his pocket, and the minute he landed he reached inside for more. After Bryce died, he started sneaking them in the air.

After Bryce, no one ever saw Bob without a fresh pack.

———•———

If they were based in the Bush, flying out of a place like St. Mary's or Aniak or Bethel or Kotzebue, then they flew with a specific set of habits. Out there it was about the snow and the ice and the wind. It was also about illusions, about pretending you could see when you couldn't and accepting that no one else could see either. They learned to trust one another in those places, or at least to trust every sane guy and avoid the ones who were nuts. Mostly though, they just learned to hate it.

Tony flew in the Bush years before anyone else. Scott served occasional weeks in the Y-K Delta, and Frank spent months convinced his bosses in Bethel were determined to kill him; they nearly succeeded. Bob did time in Bethel also, stationed there temporarily for the Company, as did Sam, who was stuck there longer than anyone else. He hated village life. Sam was so bored in Bethel that he nearly lost his mind.

Bethel was a "damp" village then, which meant you could import liquor or brew it yourself, but you couldn't buy or sell any within the city limits. No bars, no clubs, no comfortable tried-and-true chances to meet girls. Sam spent way too much time at way too many pilot house parties trying to persuade a girl, any girl, to go out on a date. These evenings usually ended up with someone's brother, cousin, friend, or former boyfriend taking a swing at him. And everyone was drunk. For a village that didn't allow the sale of alcohol, Bethel overflowed with it, and Sam was always getting into trouble. He begged the Company to move him into Town, but instead the Bosses offered him Barrow. He was so desperate to get out that he actually went. As it turned out, Barrow was just the standard sequel to your basic village nightmare—everything the same, only colder and darker.

Later, when he talked about his time living in the Bush, Sam always tried to end his stories with a laugh. But everyone noticed that it was a hollow sound, an empty sound. It was like he still couldn't figure out a way to make it all seem funny.

They learned a new language. The earliest words were for the new hires; they called them newbies, cherries, or FNGs. These were familiar terms to everyone, echoing every war movie they had ever seen. They embraced the titles although they pretended not to, all of them recognizing the thought that they were now in some kind of combat—against the weather, the Bosses, or even one another. None of them thought the names were strange or wrong. They loved this kind of excitement in their lives; some of them were desperate for it.

Quickly other words seeped into their daily conversations. They began to scud-run, or fly low beneath the weather, and the weather itself was referred to as dogshit or worse. The planes were sleds or hos or bitches, depending on the make and model. Waiting for Anchorage Center to provide radar clearance for landing presented an entire string of words that no Outsider could hope to decipher. As Sam put it one day in Bethel, "I was in my sled at the end of the train in the racetrack waiting for the zone to pop up to a mile so Center would clear us to land. It took forever." Every pilot who heard this nodded in sympathy and agreement.

Along with the words, they also had to play the game— fly when it was legal but maybe not safe, and lie when it was illegal but definitely much safer. There was physical survival, job survival, and career survival to consider. Rarely did the three converge on any flight. They had to pick and choose which was most important and fake it when they made a mistake. Some guys figured this all out in the first day with the Company, but others never got it at all.

If they were the kind to worry, there were a lot of things to be concerned about. The planes they flew were old and tired. The exteriors were patched, the interiors stained, and in a hundred different ways each of them was suffering from some sort of neglect. They were used for hauling sled dogs and snow machines as well as any other freight that fit, and they looked it. There were a lot of things that went wrong, and flying a broken airplane quickly became part of the job, just another test of loyalty to a place too cheap to do things right.

Cylinders blew, a magneto came loose, a turbo quit, a diaphragm fuel pump froze-up, connecting rod bolts failed, a waste gate stuck open, cylinders broke completely loose from the engine block, the trim tabs froze up, hydraulic pumps failed, and then the classic: One day Scott was flying out of Bethel and a cowling came off and disappeared into the tundra. The passengers loved that one; nothing like having the hood come off your car while you're driving down the interstate.

The worst though were instrument failures, because the pilots usually didn't realize the instruments were broken until they needed them. There was the time Sam was flying back from Anaktuvuk, VFR in a single-engine, when the ceiling dropped down on him and he couldn't see a thing. He punched up blind through the clouds, aiming for an altitude that was five hundred feet above the highest mountain, and that was where he stayed until he was talking to Fairbanks Approach. As he was landing though, he realized there was something wrong with the altimeter. It was off by one thousand feet. Sam actually flew home five hundred feet *below* the highest mountain along his route. Lesson learned: Never trust your altimeter; although in this case he had no idea what else he would have done.

"What the hell were my choices up there?" he asked us later. "You can't see a damn thing, and mountains in all directions. What could I do?"

"Don't fly to Anaktuvuk if there's clouds," said Tony, trying to look serious.

"Yeah, right, I'll just go out on all those perfect CAVU days this winter, like waiting for those miracles won't get me fired." Sam thought for a minute and then said, "This job is going to kill me, you know; it is totally going to kill me."

"You're a lucky son of a bitch," said Scott. "You know that?"

Sam shook his head, "I gotta start praying; I need to get religion."

"Get God or get drunk, either way you're still flying tomorrow."

And that was the bitch of it. Whatever happened today was over and tomorrow was still coming, no way to duck or hide. Tomorrow was always coming.

—·—

There were pitot tubes that clogged with ice, killing the airspeed indicator and forcing them to guess how fast they were going. Windshield heat failed, leaving them behind a sheet of ice. Prop heat failed, and the prop iced up or the deicing boots got so buried under ice that the leading edge of the wing looked like the rim of a margarita. Again and again and again, ice built up on the wings and the tail, and no matter how hard they tried to climb out of it, the ice dragged against them, stalling out the airplane over mountains and tundra and God knows what else.

Scott once flew one of the singles for thirty solid minutes with the stall indicator intermittently going off over the White Mountains. Lowering the nose increased the speed and stopped the stall, but as soon as he dropped it the slightest bit, he lost altitude and the plane wanted to keep going down. So he held it just right until he landed in Arctic Village and then pulled out a credit card and started chipping away at the inch and half of ice all over his airplane. When I asked him later how bad it got, he shook his head and said, "Peggy Fleming could have skated on my wings."

And everyone laughed about that for days because it really was funny, wasn't it?

Slowly, without realizing it, their comfort zones began to slide. They learned to navigate through the shifts, accept a new set of personal standards. At first it was about limits, like when Bob only wanted to take one flight a day and Casey wanted to verify the weight of his load before he would launch. They considered these necessary rules during training, standards they were unwilling to relinquish. Then they were put on the line, and immediately everything changed. You had to be fast and you had to be ready or you weren't going to get the flights. Before they knew it, each of them was taking off in conditions that seemed unacceptable just a few weeks before. And then, somehow, those conditions became comfortable, familiar. The zone shifted and scary became a fluid term, a dangerous gray area that was always getting grayer.

They flew in ceilings below eight hundred feet, then below five hundred, and then Tony dropped down so low over the Yukon River that water splashed on his wings. His wheels brushed the treetops on more than one occasion until, with awesome regularity, he found himself having to *climb* to clear islands or the houses at the end of the runway while on final approach into a village like Kaltag.

And he wasn't the only one.

Their visibility requirements dropped from three miles, to one mile, to maybe three thousand feet, and still they said it was flyable. Ice built up on their wings to a half-inch, and they kept flying. They flew with an inch and then collected two, all the while trying to boot it off but knowing the equipment was struggling and the deice boots were covered in ice as well. Scott hit a high point when he brought one of the Navajos in with three solid inches. If the planes could handle it, they discovered that they could as well. It was never easy, but they could do it; and after doing it for a while, they forgot all the reasons it had seemed wrong once, why it had ever seemed impossible.

They forgot everything but the last flight, the last hour on the job before they went home and got ready for the next one.

They flew fifty pounds overweight the first time and were angry about it. Then they took one hundred pounds more and then two hundred. In the single-engines they routinely went three hundred over and in the twins, five hundred. One summer day on a charter in a Navajo, Tony blew everyone's mind when he brought three thousand pounds of salmon roe back from Kaltag plus a single passenger who weighed in easily at three hundred pounds himself. The Company wasn't thrilled because if Tony had split the load and flown it legally as two flights, it would have earned the Owners twice as much. The customer gave him a hundred-dollar tip though, worth two hours of flight time. So if flying heavy got you done for the day sooner and the plane could handle it, then why not do it? Why not see just how heavy you could go? After a while, once everyone had done it over and over, there was no reason to ever stop.

It didn't take long for them to get jaded. They looked for telltale signs of pilot error in newspaper articles about crashes, began to see the unwritten things other pilots did wrong, all the things they should have done right. They could assess blame from a paragraph, a few sentences, or even less. A pilot trying to beat bad weather and losing—this was clear in a second. A pilot worrying more about giving tourists a good time than staying clear of glaciers—this was evident right away. Overloaded, loaded wrong, not enough gas, not enough brains. Every crash was avoidable, every one preventable. And they knew that every dead pilot would be replaced in days by someone desperate for the same chance that had been squandered, for the golden opportunity to prove they were better. They stopped being surprised when it happened all over again. Some weren't even surprised that much by Bryce, only that it was Bryce and that it was into the river and that the weather was good and that he died.

Bryce was one of theirs; being surprised by his crash seemed like the right thing to do.

———•———

Everyone lied to them. The Company lied from the very beginning, promising higher paychecks, bigger airplanes, and a better schedule. Some of them actually volunteered to go to the Bush because the Bosses said it was the fastest way to career advancement. Once they were out there though, they were marooned, stuck hundreds of miles from civilization flying pieces of shit in and out of one godforsaken place after another. They called the Company constantly at first, asking for a timetable back to town, trying to get someone to commit to something concrete. But all they heard were the same pointless promises over and over again.

Sometimes Sam would tell everyone about the last flight into Barrow from Fairbanks, about the cold Dominos pizzas the Bosses put onboard for him as reward if he pulled off yet another miracle. Sometimes he left them outside for the ravens and watched while they tore the boxes apart, spreading cardboard all over the ramp. Lousy pizzas. And Tony and Frank and Scott nodded their heads, all of them think-ing about cold burgers or greasy buckets of KFC that had been their rewards. Shit you bought teenagers who cleaned their rooms or got straight A's on their report card; that was what they were working for at the outstations, the approval of assholes who treated them like children.

But they ate it anyway, because at least it was something.

The village agents lied about the weather. Some of them just didn't know what they were doing when asked how the conditions were, but a lot of them lied because they wanted the plane to come in no matter what. They were expect-ing freight or mail for themselves or had someone onboard who needed to be home, and so they told the Company that the weather was good. And so the pilot launched and then found out somewhere along the route that it was total shit and he couldn't see fifty feet in front of the airplane. Usually he kept going, because he was already more than halfway and it was easier just to go, dump the load, and leave than return to the base and wait for the weather to improve. But he was pissed. So the pilot yelled at the agent and the agent lied and said he told the Company it was lousy, and the pilot went back and yelled at Ops and Ops said the agent told them it was good, and the end result was that whatever the agent wanted he got and Ops was glad to have the stuff gone and the pilot got paid. If he pulled this off enough, the agents would start to brag about him. For a while Frank was called "Ninja Pilot" because he would fly virtually blind. He squashed that nickname as quick as he could though; it was the last thing he wanted the Feds to hear.

Ops almost always lied about the load, even when they didn't have to. Every pilot was given a load manifest for his flight prior to departure. It listed everybody and everything onboard the airplane along with their weights and destination. When they were newbies they ran the calculations, made sure all the numbers worked out to a legal load, and went on their way without checking the plane. But after a few weeks with the Company, they began to notice things. There would be a dozen boxes of mail onboard for Nulato, but no Nulato mail was listed on the manifest. They would arrive in Kaltag and the agent would ask for freight. They would look in the nose compartment and there it was, but it wasn't listed on the manifest either. Cases of beer for Last Chance Liquor in Koyukuk were supposed to weigh five hundred pounds, but when they unloaded them they realized there was more like eight hundred pounds onboard. One truck tire for the Company office in Galena would turn out to be two hidden behind the back seat. A dozen pumpkins for Ruby School weighing one hundred pounds were really thirty pumpkins weighing God knows what. It went on and on and on.

Sometimes pilots would complain and, to prove a point, might throw a few things off onto the ramp before they left. On one trip Tony had the Galena ramp crew remove every single thing from his plane and weigh it when he landed there, just so he could call Ops and bitch. The Bosses apologized at first, pretended to be shocked, but after a while there was no need even for that. You just knew the load was suspect, and it was up to you to refuse it or not. And refusing, well, that might lead to time in the penalty box. Ops would either schedule you exclusively in the worst piece of crap the Company flew (like 1MD, which was slow and had a notoriously shitty cabin heater), or you just weren't scheduled at all for a few days. Pretty quickly you realized it was the way the system worked; you might hate it, but no one had any choice. Pilots flew the load because it was their job, and Ops moved the freight and mail and passengers out the door because that was theirs. Lies were just the currency that kept everyone flying and, most importantly, kept the Company paying.

In spite of all the hazards, every company had a pilot like Casey who refused to worry. He would sail past Bob, standing on the ramp desperately sucking down a cigarette and checking out the clouds, and jump into the cockpit of his single-engine airplane and be long gone while Bob was still thinking about taking off in a twin. Casey rolled every airplane the Company had and excelled at flying through ice and snow and in temperatures that were just plain crazy. One time he was stuck in Galena with a broken heater, and the mechanic the Company sent down finally had to give up; no way to fix it without more parts. So Casey straps the guy in, climbs into the left seat and tells him not to talk and fog the windshield up. Then they fly for an hour and a half back to Fairbanks. It was fifty-two below zero, and that's straight temperature, no wind chill. The mechanic didn't stop shaking for a week. But that was Casey; cold wasn't going to stop him from his date that night. Nothing was ever going to stop him.

There was this picture-perfect summer day once, and Casey was flying the Owner's visiting cousin on a cakewalk tour flight up to Anaktuvuk along with the mail. He was going up the John River, just above treetop level looking for moose and talking up all the sights to this poor dumb woman from Connecticut who never hurt a fly and had no idea that her pilot was pretty much going to get them killed if he wasn't more careful.

The John runs through canyons—lots of deep, twisting canyons—and it is okay to follow it. Hell, everybody runs it in bad weather, but you have to know when to start climbing and what turns to follow. Casey didn't worry about those things though. He was too busy thinking about how much she was loving the flight and all the good things she was going to say about him and the size of the tip she just might be sliding in his direction if he gave her that sideways grin of his often enough. And she might have been near fifty but she was good looking, so he wasn't having any trouble flirting.

Then after a while he finally started climbing out of the canyon. It didn't take him long to realize though that he was in trouble. Any pilot can do basic math, especially the kind of distance versus altitude versus side of mountain impact crater formula. Casey never would have admitted any of this to anyone, but Scott was flying out there that day, and he could see Casey was in trouble and started talking to him over the radio. He told him to pour on the power and pull the nose back hard, and all Casey could say over and over again was "I'm not going to make it; I'm not going to make it."

"You just need to pull that sucker back, hold off the stall, and you'll be fine."

"I don't think so man, I don't think it's gonna make it."

"That plane has more power than you might think. It's a good plane; it'll do it."

"Oh shit," said Casey as the mountain got closer. "Does it look good from there? Does it look good?"

"You're fine, you're great. You'll clear it easy. Just keep the nose back, and don't let up on that power."

And then they held their breath, both of them, Scott watching out his window as the little Piper Saratoga struggled to get over the trees at the top of the ridgeline. He said later that Casey cleared the mountain by fifty feet, tops. By ten o'clock that night though, he was kicking back beers, laughing his ass off, and picking up the new waitress at Pike's. And that woman who was with him? She gave Casey $50 and her phone number. She never knew he almost killed her.

———•———

So this is how it happened with Bryce:

He was leaving Tanana in a Navajo, loaded with freight and mail but no passengers. It was a clear summer morning, and he probably took off thinking about nothing but his next stop. Maybe he was looking out the window admiring the view, enjoying the quiet. Then a couple of minutes after takeoff something quit, something failed; some system or some component ceased to operate, and then he was saying he was in trouble and turning back for the airport and not making it and crashing in the Yukon. And then Bryce was dead and no one will ever know how it happened.

Witnesses heard Bryce say on the radio that he had a problem; they heard the plane hit the trees; they heard it smash into the river. They said it was sudden and sharp; they said it was like an explosion. They said they had never heard anything like it in all of their lives, and they all agreed how loud it was and how strange the quiet was that came behind it. And then they said nothing and there was only blessed silence, no more words to distract from what was Bryce's death. There were just the Company pilots, all of them, one after another, standing on the banks of the Yukon or flying low over the shore and each of them wondering what had gone wrong. "It was beautiful out there that day," Frank said later, "if only you didn't know what the river was hiding."

If only Bryce weren't dead, and if only we weren't stuck with never knowing why.

———•———

If you asked them, they would all say that the last bush pilots died long ago and they were just guys doing a job. Most of them claimed they stayed with the Company to build flight time, to advance their careers, to get a shot with the majors. Some of them said it was all about the money. Not one of them would say he had something to prove. All of them were liars.

The truth is that their mothers abandoned them when they were children, their fathers were overbearing authority figures, their wives left them, girlfriends cheated on them, siblings overshadowed their accomplishments, and no one, absolutely no one, ever understood them. They came for a thousand different reasons, but they stayed for only one: Not one of them had anywhere else to go.

By the time he left Alaska, Sam held more than a dozen names in his memory, all of whom died while flying. Some of them were particularly dear; a few were irreplaceable. He wondered though about the ones he didn't have names for, the ones he didn't even know were gone. "How many guys did I talk to on the radio, did I see on the ramp in Barrow or Bethel or have lunch with in McGrath during fire season, that just aren't here anymore?" he asked one night. "How many of those guys I kind of knew but can't remember are gone now? I mean, do I really know fifteen dead pilots, or do I know thirty or forty?

"How many do any of us know?"

And for a minute, sitting over after-work beers at Pike's, we realized that together we might fill the room with our dead; we might fill the entire restaurant. There could be a hundred dead pilots we knew; there could be more. We found ourselves shocked at the thought, lost for words as we looked at the tables and chairs surrounding us and considered the faces that could have been there.

And then we all started talking at once. Because the honest answer is that we didn't know how many names there were, and on a good night we didn't care. On a good night we didn't even remember Bryce. But the truth was, there were never enough good nights, and everyone knew it.

We didn't tell anyone that though, not even each other.

2

The Question of Why

To understand Alaskans, you first need to know that it is not about where they came from but why they decided to leave there in the first place. Everyone travels north because they want something from it: a new job, a new hope, a new future. Alaska, by dint of geography and persistent mythology, is the place of far, far away. The people who go there for redemption, resurrection, or a place to hide forever make sure that critical part of it never changes. They make sure the Last Frontier stays at the end of the farthest road.

For all their own reasons, they need it to be that kind of place.

In 1922 Ben Eielson accepted a teaching contract in Fairbanks. He was a Midwesterner who had come from a background of storekeeping, civility, and college. It was not a childhood that bred daring young men, and yet there he was. He learned to fly in 1917 in the Army Air Service and received sailing orders for Europe, but the armistice was signed before he departed. Like so many others, Eielson found himself a pilot without a plane. In the years that followed he drifted from one career attempt to another, trying to find a way to make a living in the air or on the ground. None of them stuck until he took the job in Fairbanks and found a place that was surprisingly eager to help him fly.

The Alaskan newspapers were full of aviation stories from around the world; any chance to talk about flying found its way into local conversation and print. Eielson had fallen into the perfect place for an aviator looking for another chance. He became friends with the editor of the *Fairbanks Daily News-Miner,* and together they persuaded the city to put up the money for a plane. He made good use of the Curtiss Jenny when it arrived in 1923, but it could only carry him so far, and Eielson was somebody who had big dreams.

Little flights weren't enough for him. His first step toward creating the bush pilot legend was through the award of the earliest airmail contract in Alaska in late 1923. No winter flights had ever been made in the territory; there were no accurate maps, and daylight was fleeting at best. But Eielson was determined to succeed and knew that successfully delivering the mail was the fastest way to do that. Through one accident and near catastrophe after another, he didn't give up. He thought Alaska could become the center of a new aviation world, and he was determined to be part of it. He was in fact on his way to being essential to its success.

He just had to fly blind through the dark and the snow and the cold to do it.

———◦———

I came to Alaska in the hopes of leaving aviation behind
forever. I had a degree in it, I had my private pilot's license,
and I had experience working for one of the busiest airports
in the country. I also hated everything about fielding noise
complaints and filing community meeting reports and the
cutthroat nature of office politics. Aviation had quickly
become just like any other job, nothing exciting, nothing
special. Working for a Bush airline in Alaska offered not
only a radical change in geography but also the promise of
capturing a living page of history from aviation's golden age.
I didn't want to cross the top of the world, but I didn't mind
a shot at seeing it.

A year after I moved to Fairbanks I was hired at the
Company as a dispatcher in the Ops department. I was part
of every departure, arrival, load, and route. I knew all the
pilots and mechanics, what planes were slower, which ones
were colder, and which one no one ever wanted to fly. I was
on the ramp organizing loads and in the office talking to the
post office, the FAA, and the competition. The passengers
were my friends, the pilots my family. But it didn't take long
to realize that I would never do anything at the Company
other than get the flights off the ground. I wasn't building
flight time for a better job or angling for a move up the
seniority line so that I could get a bigger paycheck. Lead
dispatch was the best job I was going to get there.

I spent four years with my eyes on the front door watching the wannabes come in chasing the tail of Eielson's

dream, even though most of them didn't know his name. They all had that same rush going on, that firm conviction that this would be the place where their careers would take off. But for all the pilots who came up from Outside, there was always someone left behind; someone who didn't like the idea of big chances or wasn't so sure about flying in the cold. Someone who thought they were a fool or worse. That voice was always there in the back of their heads or their hearts and didn't let them go. It was why they had something to prove even when the rest of us didn't care.

What they left behind was nearly always part of why they came through that door.

The one thing I had in common with those new pilots was coming from someplace else. The Company was how we lived, but someplace else was what we knew. And years in Alaska, even decades, wouldn't change that. You always bring home with you. No matter how desperately you want to leave it behind, you always bring home with you wherever you go.

Impossibly, not even one month after I went to work for the Company, there was a fatality crash. The pilot was someone none of us knew, flying for the competition. He was a newbie and flew his single-engine into the side of Atigun Pass on a day when he was warned to not even attempt a flight through it. What went wrong was obvious nearly from the moment it happened; an inexperienced pilot chose the wrong route and then stayed with his bad choice too long. He took off in a bad direction, he continued flying it when the weather was clearly shit, and he hit a mountain. There was no question of anything other than pilot error.

In the days after the accident, as the route was hashed out and everyone had their say, it never got easier to understand why he made such obvious mistakes. He was on the last legs of a long flight and stopped in several villages before reaching Galbraith Lake. Galbraith is a private strip built by the oil companies that pretty much only exists for dropping off crews and supplies. He got to Galbraith by flying through Anaktuvuk Pass, which is the normal route through the Brooks Range. He was supposed to fly from there back to the village of Bettles and then to Fairbanks. But he told a pilot on the ground in Galbraith that he was going direct to Fairbanks through Atigun Pass. The second pilot told the Feds later he advised against that; the weather was bad and the newbie admitted he didn't know Atigun Pass well. But he insisted he wanted to check it out anyway, even after the second guy told him someone else had just tried less than an hour earlier and turned back.

This was classic pilot error, the kind of accident that makes the Feds annoyed to even have to do the paperwork. Everyone called it from the beginning, and everyone was right. But what no one could explain was why he made that stupid decision—why he decided to fly into a pass he was unfamiliar with that was partially obscured by clouds. Why did he take his VFR self into IMC? Why go die when there were other ways to go live?

What made Atigun Pass this guy's best choice?

He was twenty-six years old when he died. His company said he had over twelve hundred hours, although they couldn't say how much of it was PIC or even how much instrument time he had. He probably lied about his hours;

told them what they wanted to hear so he could get hired. But even if all that time was his, he was clearly out of his depth in the Brooks Range, beyond his ability and way over his head. So he made a bad decision and it killed him. But thinking about it now, I can see the first step that kid took toward dying was long before Galbraith Lake. It was back when he came to Alaska, when he believed that luck would see him through, when he convinced himself that taking chances with the mountains was a reasonable thing to do. And why he thought that idea was right is the question no one can ever seem to answer.

I guess the bigger question is why Eielson flew into those canyons when no one knew how to get out of them and lived and this kid, who had all the maps in the world, managed to die. Did he bring his bad luck with him, or did he choose it that day on the ramp in Galbraith? Was he ever going to live to fly another day even without Alaska, or was he cruising for a crash the moment he soloed, the moment he showed himself to be a pilot who wanted to take a look even when looking was the most dangerous decision he could make?

Why do some pilots live and some die?

—·—

Sam Beach and I talk sometimes. We start with his job; he's flying in the Lower 48 now. We talk about our families, the people and places we know together. And then finally we talk about the Company, which is what we wanted to talk about all along but never know how to start.

Lately he is asking about what I'm writing, how I'm planning to fit his story into it. He's worried about parts of it, about late-night phone calls when he thought he was losing it, about showing up at my door one day after too long in the Bush with no end in sight, about all the times I know he almost crashed.

"Don't make me sound weak," he says, and I have to shake my head. How could anyone who flew those kinds of hours in that kind of weather ever look weak?

"You're the hero of the whole thing," I say, and we laugh.

"The guy still standing at the end," he says.

"Steve McQueen in *The Great Escape*."

"He didn't get out though," says Sam.

"But he lived," I remind him.

"And he didn't go crazy," he adds and then looks at me shaking his head. "I don't know how you're going to write this book."

———•———

There are thousands of stories about snow or fog, flying tired, flying cold, or even flying blind. Telling them is as common as telling cold weather survival stories, or I-shot-a-moose stories, or I-was-charged-by-a-bear-and-nearly-died stories. In 1996 a book called *Cowboys of the Sky* was published full of stories about bush pilots doing outrageous things. They are mostly from the old days though, because only dead people would admit to that sort of thing.

Every chapter has a different hero. In the 1930s an Alaskan Southern Airways pilot brought a body in from Dutch

Harbor and "strapped the corpse onto the top of the wing." In 1949 pilot Archie Ferguson couldn't quite fit a boiler into his plane, so he "chopped a hole in the roof of the Fairchild and flew it with the stovepipe sticking through the top of the airplane." In the 1950s Jack Jefford was in serious weather when he got pulled into a downdraft and felt "an awful jar on the airplane." He eased the power back and eventually turned the engine off, only to discover after the weather cleared that he was "perched on a mountaintop." Author Steven Levi said these men were "the stuff from which legends were made."

"How about that," I tell Sam about the book, looking for a joke. "You were a cowboy."

"So was Steve McQueen more than once," he reminds me. But then, "Don't make it just about the wild stuff, the stupid shit," he says. "You know it was mostly just flying, nothing special."

"You don't want to be a hero?"

"I don't think any of them wanted to be heroes," he says.

"But that doesn't explain why they took their chances."

"Nope," he agrees. "And it doesn't explain why I took mine either."

The problem with Alaska flying stories is that to understand them you have to start at the beginning. You have to go back to the guys who were flying here in the 1920s and did some crazy stuff, partly because they had to and partly because you had to be a little bit crazy in order to want to fly in Alaska in the 1920s in the first place.

Of course Ben Eielson is in *Cowboys of the Sky*, along with that first bush mail flight and the first trans-Arctic flight he completed with George Wilkins in 1928. The reason practically no one beyond Eielson Air Force Base knows anything about him is that in aviation terms he's ancient history. He and his mechanic disappeared in late 1929 while flying a very lucrative contract to transport furs and passengers from an icebound ship, the *Nanuk,* off the Siberian coast to Fairbanks. Their bodies were found three months later in Siberia, cementing Eielson's tragic fame. Alaskans proclaimed him a hero, said he died to bring aviation to the North and decided that kind of dying was something pilots were just going to have to be willing to do to get the job done. Even if Eielson might one day be forgotten, his flying was going to live forever.

By the time Eielson disappeared in November, the search for fellow pilot Russ Merrill was over. Merrill vanished on a clear September day in 1929 on a scheduled run out of Anchorage hauling freight and mail. In his case a body was never found, and there are only theories about a forced landing in the water (he was flying a floatplane). No one knows where he fell out the sky, let alone why. His story is not about a rescue or big contracts but rather the tedious maintenance of the schedule. Merrill had been up for thirteen hours that last day and flown for eight when he departed Anchorage again with a freight delivery. If he had made it to his planned first stop in Sleetmute, he would have ended up flying around eleven hours in a fifteen-hour workday. He was willing to do this because his customers mattered to him and because, as his son later wrote in his biography, ". . . meeting his schedule was uppermost in his mind."

Eielson was part of the search for Merrill until the *Nanuk* contract drew him away. The only thing that was ever found of his friend was a small piece of fabric that matched Merrill's wing. It washed up on a beach on the west side of Cook Inlet where the Natives recalled seeing something floating far out to sea around the time of his disappearance. It might have been Merrill or it might have been nothing, but it was the only ending to that story anyone ever got.

"We never knew who they were," says Sam. "We never sat around talking about Eielson or Merrill. They were just names on buildings or road signs; more dead guys. Who talks about Charles Lindbergh anyway outside of a museum?"

"But you flew like they did," I reminded him. "More than sixty years later it was still them flying out there."

"We flew the way the Bosses wanted," he corrected.

"Same thing."

And he knew it was.

———————

The most important thing I know about Alaska aviation is that you can't be a part of it if you aren't willing to tell the story later. You have to commit to that; you have to bring yourself to the table and tell everyone what you know. It's been that way since the beginning; the bush pilots are legends for a reason. According to the myths, the bigger story of Alaskan aviation, pilots don't crash in Alaska because they are foolish or crazy or stupid, and they never have—not to anyone who matters. They've always been brave in the Far North; they've always been courageous. That's what we knew about Ben Eielson and Russ Merrill in 1929, and it's still what we know today.

But the things I remember, they aren't those things. In my head the phone is ringing the day Bryce crashed, and that moment before I answered, before I knew he was gone, is still a moment I keep. I remember Sam coming back after six months in Barrow and walking through the Company on the way home to his parents like he didn't even know me, like he didn't know any of us. I remember a knock on the door, and just like that my friend John is dead. On his snow machine crossing a highway and there was a truck, and John didn't see it; the guy in the truck didn't see him. And we couldn't believe it; none of us could believe it.

You never expect a pilot to die on the ground, but mostly you just never expect so many things to go wrong, and to keep going wrong over and over again. You never expect the crashing or the dying.

We talked about leaving Alaska all the time; it was a conversation that was so common it was like a hobby. We sat around at Pike's drinking beer and eating burgers and wandered in and out of talking about how much better we thought our lives would be after we left the Company. We made plans for big houses and fast cars; about living in a city, going to shows and shopping malls. We daydreamed our way through one year after another, always saying it wasn't going to be much longer, it wasn't going to last forever; always saying we could leave at anytime.

And Casey said it was all just fun while he reached for one more of Bob's cigarettes, and Frank said it was important work while he ordered two more beers before the drive home, and Scott said it was just a job while he didn't notice that his wife packed her bags and left him. Tony kept renting apartments even though he had lived in Alaska his whole life. Every year Sam was stationed farther and farther away, and Bryce asked for more flights—no matter how many hours he worked at his day job—always crafting his master plan to get the most cash and flight time and get out for good.

He was the one who knew what he wanted.

All of us sat there telling our lies and playing our game of pretend and knowing that at least none of us would ask the questions we didn't want to answer because all of us owned those same questions. Together we were happy because together we were understood. We stayed because we had no choice; there was no choice for any of us but the Company.

At least there we weren't alone; the best thing about the Company was that none of us were ever alone.

———•———

"Fifty guys died in that escape," says Sam.

"Not Steve McQueen," I remind him. "He didn't die."

"He was fiction," says Sam. "His character wasn't based on anyone who was really in that camp. Even the damn motorcycle was fiction."

"That's not the point though. He made it."

"They all wanted to live," he says.

"I know," I tell him, and I'm thinking about Bryce. I don't know who Sam is thinking about.

"You'll tell some of the dying?" he asks me.

"Some of it," I agree. To tell it right, I have to tell some of the dying.

"But make sure it has a happy ending," he says. "That's what I tell myself, that this is the happy ending."

And I tell him, yeah, of course I will. What we're living now, that's our happy ending, or at least the best ending that any of us could expect.

Here are some good stories: Standing on the ramp in the morning watching the sun come up and it's quiet and the planes aren't loaded yet and nothing's screwed up and we're all looking forward to what comes next. Laughing when Casey and his date get caught in the ladies bathroom by the waitresses at Pike's. Watching the guys overload the Islander until the tail stand hits the ground because Scott dares them to; calling the tower to ask for priority clearance because we have a pilot coming in alone with a single passenger onboard well on her way to having a baby. If I close my eyes right now I can still see Casey standing in Ops singing along to the radio.

These are short stories, two seconds on the page, but they changed my life. The Company was more than broken airplanes, lousy weather, and trying not to die. It was stories

I can't forget even now; it was Company stories that saved me and Sam and Scott and Tony and everyone else. Company stories that keep Bryce alive.

It might have been seventy years ago, but the only reason Eielson and Merrill are still with us is because their stories wouldn't go away either. And the same is true of Steve McQueen.

3

On the Ramp

Aviation isn't all dangerous in Alaska, and it isn't all glory. Funny things happened all the time at the Company, wild and crazy things. A guy shows up one morning with a truckload of Kentucky bloodhounds that just came in from the Lower 48, and they have to be loaded up in a Navajo for a bunch of hunters who are waiting on them downriver in Kaltag. So everyone's standing out on the ramp and Cargo Bill and Shawn are looking at each other and these dogs and knowing they need to get them loaded up and out of there before the whole day is screwed up but how to do that, how to get these dogs, which are not sled dogs and have no clue what they're supposed to do, into the airplane is purely a mystery. Then all twelve of them just start howling like they've got the scent of the biggest bear that was ever born. And there's no way you could make anyone believe that it all ever happened, that Kentucky bloodhounds would be howling at the planes as they taxied by at dawn on the ramp in Fairbanks, Alaska.

But it's true, and I was there to see it.

———•———

Tony had a flight out of Tanana when his left engine caught on fire right after takeoff. He put the fire out and got the plane down, but when he looks at the wing, you know what was floating down all over the runway?

Tampons; thousands of tampons.

"All the mail in the left nacelle was boxes of tampons," said Tony, "and they burned up in the fire and were floating down all over the place, so on top of everything else I'm stuck standing on the runway picking half-baked tampons up off the ground while everyone points and laughs.

"And how was your day?" he always asked next.

———•———

At fifty below zero everyone started thinking long and hard about flying. If we decided to go downriver and the competition didn't, then we could get all the mail for the downriver villages transferred to us. The Owners liked that idea.

"Pull up 2KD," they said, "just in case."

Fifteen minutes after we moved our Beech 99, the competition pulled theirs up as well.

Shit.

"Get the heat on it," the Bosses said.

The cargo guys came up front, bundled in Carhartts, scarves, parkas, and fur. "They've got the heat on too," they said. Now it was getting fun.

The post office called and told us to transfer our mail to the competition. "We're going," I told them. "We've got the heat on right now," I said. "They can see it from next door."

Now the post office would have to split everyone else's mail between the two of us. We were going to roll out at the same time. Galena called; it was fifty-five below.

The whole way downriver Frank and Casey talked to the competition. Not one of them wanted to be out there, and they were still trying to figure out why they were.

"Why did you guys have to pull up?" Frank asked.

"So we could be ready if you guys did,"

"But we weren't going to go until you looked like you were going."

"Well, if you weren't going then we wouldn't have had to go."

Back and forth for over an hour, and nobody could figure out why either flight was in the air.

In Galena it was just like Fairbanks, boxes passed from hand to hand, sacks thrown down on the ground. After they unloaded, they drank hot coffee in the office. The seats on the plane were frozen hard as rocks, their sandwiches were cold; Casey couldn't feel his face. They loaded up outgoing mail and taxied out to leave; the competition was right behind them.

Flying out of Galena the radio was quiet. Then a voice came on announcing traffic into the nearby village of Huslia.

Frank and the competition called back to him right away. "What are you guys doing out here?" the third pilot, a guy who flew for Eastern Airlines in his previous life and was one of the best on the ramp, asked them.

"Us? What the hell are *you* doing out here?" Frank asked. The other guy was the chief pilot for a smaller carrier on the ramp and he was flying a single-engine.

"What do you think I'm doing? You fly, they fly; I get a phone call from the post office and I've got to fly to stay in business."

His company opted not to transfer their mail; they decided to try and deliver it.

"You stay out here and we're going to be reading about you in the papers tomorrow," said Frank.

"Then I'll be famous."

They left him behind as he headed into Huslia, the turbines flying home at 170 knots and his single hanging in there at 140.

The next day it was still fifty below. We were in the office, playing that game again where we fantasized about working for an airline in the South Pacific. The competition wasn't pulling their plane up; neither were we.

This time around we weren't even pretending that we might.

Everyone was talking about the little three-paragraph story in the *News-Miner*. That single-engine plane got into Huslia, but its fuel pump quit after departure. He went down in a slough outside the village. The plane and pilot were fine—so fine in fact that he pulled the Huslia mail that was bound for Fairbanks out of the nose compartment before he left the plane. As long as he was the first one out with it, the money was still for his company when he brought it into Town.

He called us the next morning at ten o'clock. "Come and get me and I'll buy the beer tonight," he promised.

We didn't have to go but he was real—he was permanent. A lot of those guys might be around for just a year or two, but with him you were talking Alaska forever. Frank and Casey went out again and brought the newspaper along so that the first thing he had to do when he climbed into 2KD was sign it. It went up on our bulletin board that afternoon and stayed there for years.

But he didn't care because the mail he brought with him was still his.

—————

Fire season added a different spin to our mornings. During summer when the Interior was burning, we would gather on the ramp, checking the hills for signs of smoke. Fire meant round-the-clock charters to carry equipment and firefighters. It meant free meals and no rules, and most importantly it meant money.

"What do you see out there today?" Scott would ask looking north.

"The radio says half the state is on fire," I said.

"Burn baby, burn," laughed Frank, taking a drag from his cigarette.

"Fuck yeah," agreed Scott, "fuck yeah."

We loved fire season.

There was the newbie who got lost on the way to Venetie and went back to Beaver to ask for a volunteer to fly along and show him the way—and then didn't understand when the Bosses were pissed.

The newbie who only wanted to fly in clear weather and quit when one of the Bosses flew alongside him and made it clear that in Alaska he had to fly in snow.

The newbie copilot who Scott wrote up as "inop" when he refused to fly home from Galena because he had a headache.

The pilot who needed one of the Bosses to start the Navajo for him in the morning more than once because he kept flooding the engine.

The pilot who got cold in Galena and refused to fly home.

The one whose wife left him and he refused to fly because he missed her too much.

The one who got so drunk the night before he was scheduled to fly copilot for a captain's check ride that he was still drunk the next morning. And then threw up on final approach.

The one who flew with his dog in the copilot seat.

The ones who got scared and the ones who got angry and the ones who just went away, never to be heard from again.

If I close my eyes I can see us standing in Ops absently singing along to a bluesy Tracy Chapman song about having a reason to stay. A busted-up love song as the Company anthem. What I don't know is if the song was about leaving or how we all got there in the first place. It doesn't really matter though; it was what we heard over and over getting ready in the morning, trying to make the flights on time, trying not to freeze to death in the process. Before we knew it, it was our theme song; it was the one that made sense.

I can still remember Tony coming back from every single Mount McKinley flight-seeing flight and his passengers going on and on about how spectacular the mountain was to see. I ask him how come the mountain is never clouded in when he's flying, and he laughs and says the trick isn't finding Denali on a good day but any mountain on a bad one.

And then there's my friend Jen Nelson who told a story about flying a King Air one day for the competition into Barrow on a school charter to pick up the Anaktuvuk girls basketball team. One of the girls showed up at the office with a frozen dead seal that weighed in at about 120 pounds; it was her excess baggage. Sam was running the base then, and he and his cargo guy pulled that thing over to the lower cargo compartment, the pod, under the plane. The animal was too round to slide in and too frozen to slip in. So they sat down and used their feet to force it in. Once it got through the door it fit like it had been inside the pod forever. Then they jammed a bunch of other stuff around it. Sam had no idea how they were going to get it all out in Anaktuvuk, but he didn't really care either. His problem was Barrow, and as far as he was concerned, nowhere else existed.

There were some guys with ropes waiting when they arrived in the village. Jen popped the belly pod open, and then she and her copilot got to work yanking the seal out. They manhandled it without much damage and then handed it over to the family, who tied it up and walked down the ramp pulling the seal across the snow behind them.

"You've flown something weirder than that?" I asked her later.

"I've flown some seriously weird shit," said Jen.

"What's the weirdest?"

"Head in a box."

"What do you mean, 'head in a box'?"

"I flew a guy back from Kaktovik once," she said. "He had a box and it leaked. I asked him what was in the box and he said it was a head. Left a nice puddle of something behind on the floorboards by the time we got to Town."

"A head from what?"

"I didn't ask."

"It could have been a human head you know."

"Kaktovik is a small village," said Jen shaking her head; "they would notice if someone's head was missing. I would have heard about it."

Sometimes, she told me, it was better just not to ask any questions.

———·———

Scott came back from Galena one day after being stuck on the ground for a couple of hours with a flat tire. His passenger wanted to get home to Kaltag and bitched about the delay because he thought Scott should change the tire himself. It wasn't doing any good to explain the whole federal regulations requirement for a licensed mechanic. The passenger got more and more worked up, and Scott was sick of trying to explain; then the guy pulled a knife and started chasing him around the plane screaming that he wanted to go home. Scott was running for his life until everyone piled out of the office and got the guy to calm down.

Every time I tell it, this story makes me laugh, and everybody else laughs too. That's what flying in Alaska is like, Scott would say. A flat tire and a passenger with a knife and the Company saying well, yeah—but is the plane all right?

———•———

Here's the question you really want answered though: How cold did it get? How about twenty below with a twenty-knot crosswind in Anaktuvuk in a single and Scott couldn't see and the plane was frozen, and it was two days until he could fly out. Or forty-five below in Galena and maintenance was recovering the BE99 that spun into the snow in Ruby, and there was nowhere to hide while they did the work. It was fifty-seven below in Beaver in a Navajo when Tony flew in, and our agent Babe Adams came out and said "What the hell are you doing here?" Then it was sixty below at Fort Yukon in the BE99 and we left the right engine turning, offloaded one passenger and some freight, and got out in a three-minute turn. It was forty below with a forty-knot crosswind in the BE99 in Deadhorse with Scott and Casey, and it hurt to do everything but leave. And the biggest surprise of all, it was twenty above and I walked outside to help load in just a sweatshirt. Shawn and Bill weren't wearing coats either.

———•———

There were a thousand stories that seem unbelievable when I tell them now, even to me, but I know they are true. Like the hunters who flew out into the Bush with an espresso machine and sourdough starter for their "real wilderness experience" and the planeload of traditional Athabascan fiddlers who came in from Canada for a festival chewing on smoked salmon jerky all the way. We saw extremes everyday that seemed improbable if not impossible. If I remember the stories, then I know the life I lived was true; I know it happened; I know that once upon a time this was who we were and how we lived.

4
Onto the Ice

Sometimes the flying stories we told belonged to someone else. Scott told a story about a guy he flew with named Ray Marrs. Ray crashed off the coast of Nome with a full load of passengers; by a miracle there were no injuries, but the whole thing was a mess. The Feds went after Ray and he fought them hard, kept insisting it wasn't his fault, wasn't anybody's fault. And then one day he got real quiet, and soon after that he was gone. That's when Scott started telling his story.

From the very beginning Ray's job in Nome was a good contract for the Company—they signed over a plane and pilot to the school district for the year to transport students throughout the region. It was an unusual arrangement for a lot of reasons, but mostly because the Company had little actual control over where the plane flew or under what conditions. School officials called Ray in Nome, let him know where they needed him to be and when, and then he figured out the fuel and load and timing. He had no real oversight or supervision, even though he was supposed to. He was out in the boonies flying around and dealing directly with a customer who had paid up front for his time. It put him in a precarious position, a place where saying no would not be easy. "None of that was a problem though," said Scott later, "because Ray never liked to say no anyway."

He was the kind of guy who liked to get the job done.

"We all know he wasn't the only guy out there like that," said Scott. "Hell, he wasn't even the only one the Company had like that. It's not about the time or money for them or the big dream career down the line. Ray wanted to be talked about in the villages; he wanted people to know about him. He volunteered for Nome in the first place because he knew the job would give him that, plus he wouldn't have to listen to the Bosses much."

"You think he was looking for a legend?" asked Casey. "Trying to be the next big thing?"

"Maybe," said Scott. "Then the minute he started flying up there, he knew he was going to be it."

"Why would you care what anybody else thinks?" asked Sam.

"Because," said Bob. "Because for some guys everybody else are the only ones you have."

"Or maybe he just liked it," said Scott; "maybe he liked it all a little too much."

It was easy at first. The district called and gave him a schedule, and Ray set up the flights. He flew heavy a lot, but that wasn't unusual with the schools. They always had a ton of gear, and he ended up fudging the student weights so often that he had to keep a crib sheet of the fake weights for consistency. He didn't want kids gaining and losing fifty pounds on a weekly basis when the names were right there on the manifests and easy to track. The district knew what he was doing; they had to know what he was doing. They knew the total weight he could carry, and they could add it up. But if they thought about it all, they figured if he was willing to do it then it must be okay. The plane was fine; it was safe. Everybody flew heavy. Problem was, though, that wasn't the only corner Ray was cutting.

That anyone was surprised by this is the only thing that's hard to believe about it.

It was a long day of flying that finally got him. Go to one village and get some kids, take them to another village and drop them off, then pick up another full load and come back to Nome, get some fuel, and take those kids on to the first village. Fly in one big slow circle for most of the day. Ray planned it all out, basing his flight times on good weather. He left on time for his first leg, an empty plane except full of fuel.

At least that's what the paperwork said.

"Anyone would have tankered it, filled it to the top," said Sam. "On a long flight like that, I always do."

"The only time you have too much fuel is when you're on fire," agreed Tony. It was a cliché, but everybody still believed it.

"What did he do?" I asked.

"He was going to be heavy with passengers when he picked up his first load, and he knew it. He couldn't have full fuel out of Nome and still be legal out of Kaltag," said Scott.

"So why not go minimum fuel out of Nome, get the boys in Kaltag, and then add a stop along the way to get more fuel in Unalakleet?" asked Sam.

"That's what you would do?" asked Scott.

"That's what anyone with a brain would do," said Tony.

"He thought he could make it all the way without stopping, didn't he?" asked Bob.

"He thought he was too good to need a cushion?" I asked. "Any cushion at all?"

"Thought he was too good for everything," said Scott.

"Shit."

"Yeah, you can see it coming can't you," said Scott; "you can see it coming for him a mile away."

From Nome to Kaltag was a flight of just over an hour. Ray loaded up a heavy group of nine teenage boys on an away game to play basketball. He didn't write down their baggage, and he fudged all of their weights. Then he went out over the Bering Sea to St. Lawrence Island to drop the boys off and pick up the next full load, eight girls from Gambell. That flight was just over two hours long, with no accounting for wind. Then he headed to Nome, just over an hour, to get more fuel before going back to Kaltag to drop the girls off.

"Couldn't work," said Sam decisively, although he looked over to Tony for confirmation; Tony had more time in the Navajos than anyone.

"He could put four and a half hours of fuel max in that plane, and the flight ended up how long on paper?" asked Bob.

"Four hours and fifteen minutes, and that's strictly straight flight time, no delays in the air or on the ground with the engines running. Plus there's no cushion for sucking fuel down during takeoff."

"And we don't think he was full of fuel from the beginning anyway," said Sam, "right?"

"Yeah," said Tony. "And remember, he was flying back from St. Lawrence, and all they have is wind out there."

"He thought he could beat the wind," I said, shaking my head.

"Why shouldn't he think that?" asked Scott. "It's what everyone wanted him to think. Why else do you think the Company chose him?"

"Ask that and you have to wonder why the Bosses chose any of us," said Bob.

"There's a question no one wants answered," said Sam.

"There's a difference," said Tony. "There's pushing it, and then there's having a death wish. They aren't the same thing."

"No," agreed Scott. "Ray wasn't like us, he thought he was better."

"Better?" said Bob. "More like crazier."

"Ray thought he could beat God," said Sam.

"He thought he *was* God," said Scott.

"No, Ray just thought he could beat the airplane," said Tony shaking his head. "That's where he fucked up. No one can beat the airplane."

"But there's always someone who thinks they can," I said, "isn't there? There's always someone who has to try."

———•———

Understand this: It's not a plan. You don't leave thinking you will land with barely enough fuel; you don't time it so you taxi in on fumes. That is never the intention. It's all easy math, high school math; look at the distance, calculate the time, you know how many gallons the plane burns per hour. You know what you need to be legal, thirty minutes more than the flight unless the weather is shit, and then you need at least forty-five minutes for IFR reserves. And you know the legalities are bullshit, so you carry what you need to feel safe, which for any reasonable person means as much fuel as possible. When a full load is not enough to complete the flight, then you plan an extra stop along the way. The Company had its own fuel in Galena and accounts with companies all over the state. It is not impossible to get fuel; it was not even difficult. Fuel for a thirsty airplane is necessary, and if you don't plan for enough, then clearly you want to die. Or you're so arrogant you think you can survive anything.

———•———

"It wasn't a game, I think," said Scott. "Ray wasn't trying to get farther on less. The first time he did, it was probably an accident; maybe he ran into weather he hadn't planned for and ended up coming in on fumes. Everybody's been there at least once. He was probably coming back from a long flight. He had to fly in the shit and ran into some approach delays when he got back to Town, and just like that he was parked on the ramp and the gas gauge was reading lower than he ever thought it could go. But he made it okay, and no one had a clue how close he had been."

"And so he does it again?" asked Bob.

"Nobody does it again," said Tony.

"Well," said Scott, "maybe the second time was an accident too, but then he got cocky. He thought he knew how to handle it; he thought it was skill that got him down with no one knowing it and not dumb luck. He thought he had learned a secret."

Everyone looked at him when he said that. No one believed him. Tony even smiled.

"Or maybe he was just a fucking idiot," conceded Scott, "but I'd like to give the guy some kind of break; he was arrogant and not stupid. That's the only break he deserves."

No one said anything, but they were all thinking it: What kind of break did Ray's passengers deserve? A planeload of teenage girls going to a ballgame; where was their break?

When Ray left Gambell everything was fine. The girls were all talk in the back of the plane, and he was glad to have the engines drown them out. He said later he took a look at the gas gauges the first time when he was halfway back. He had probably looked at them before that, but this was the first time he noticed, when he really understood what the readings meant. He saw there might be a problem. Ray had been there before though; he figured he knew how far a Navajo would fly on low fuel. He did all the things you could to make the fuel last: adjusted the manifold pressure to get off the turbo, got real smooth and light on the controls to minimize drag, sought out the best altitude for the winds.

"I told you," said Scott, "he was arrogant but not stupid. He went through the right motions; he kept flying the plane. He had a plan to get it down on the ground."

"He had less than five hundred hours in the Navajo," said Tony, "and how many in that particular plane? Fifty? One hundred?"

"I didn't say it was a plan with a chance in hell of success," said Scott.

He didn't have to say that; everybody knew how Ray's plan worked out.

———•———

The left engine stalled first, and that got the girls worried but not panicked. They had lived on an island all their lives and seen a lot of flight time; they knew this kind of thing could happen. But when the second engine crapped out, they started screaming. They weren't flying over tropical waters; it was the Bering Sea outside their windows, about as cold as water can get before it turns to ice. There was no reason to try to survive a crash landing out there, and everyone knew it. You didn't live long crashing in the Bering Sea.

Ray made a perfect gear-up landing on the sea ice about seven miles off the coast. The plane bounced in hard but did not break apart. All things considered, it was a very good landing. He had made all the necessary radio calls on the way down, and the Air National Guard was there in minutes to pick them up in a helicopter. They were safe, and at first Ray looked to be a hero. He said the plane had a fuel leak and everybody who listened believed him; they wanted to believe him. Even when the Feds showed up and started asking difficult questions, Ray wasn't worried. He knew it was their job to be suspicious, but the only thing that mattered to him was what he knew was true. He believed in that fuel leak and showed no signs of doubting it.

"He was covering his ass with the Feds," said Tony. "He got caught with his pants down and said what he had to say from the beginning to try and save himself. You can't have it both ways, Scott," he added. "If he was arrogant enough to run out of gas, then he also thought he could lie his way out."

Everyone knew Tony was right. It made sense for Ray to say nothing when the Feds went looking for answers. He was no newbie; he had been around long enough to know how to play the game. The Company would never have cut him loose in Nome if they hadn't been confident of that. He needed to play dumber than dumb, but that wasn't what he decided to do. Even the Bosses were surprised when Ray started yelling about a leak. It was easy to disprove something like that when you had a fully intact airplane, very easy. Ray was going to get caught in his lie. But he wouldn't let it go. Everyone knew that his paperwork showed the flight was impossible and that his weights were off from the beginning. But still, Ray didn't give up on his story.

"After a fuckup like that, all he had was the lie," said Bob.

"The lie that he was ever good enough to do the job they gave him," said Tony.

"That's all any of us ever have," said Scott. "Haven't you figured that out yet?"

The Company grounded Ray immediately, standard operating procedure. The Feds liked that sort of thing. The plane was carefully flown back under a ferry permit (which ended up being lucky as Maintenance later found a cracked wing spar), and other than the damage from the landing, nothing was found mechanically wrong with it. The Company mechanics poured over it and so did the Feds, and they were all diligent; they were careful. They had a pilot, alive and well, swearing that it was not his fault. It was easy to call him a liar, but they had to make sure there was nothing wrong with the Navajo that could have caused the accident. Everyone spent a lot of time looking for something that was not there, but Ray never changed his story, not for a minute. He was absolutely certain the crash was not his fault.

"Can't let go of a story when you've been telling it for that long," I said.

"But Christ," said Bob, "he had to know it was making him look bad. What was he thinking?"

"He stopped thinking when he didn't refuel after the first stop," said Tony. "Or maybe," he continued, "he stopped thinking after the first time he landed with no fuel and wasn't scared enough to make sure it never happened again."

"But still, that's the one thing that never made any sense to me," said Scott. "Why did he stay with the story? Why didn't he just admit the whole thing was his fuckup, take the punishment, and go back to work?"

"Probably would have been a suspension," said Bob, "at least six months, maybe longer."

"The Company would have found something for him, running one of the out stations or working in Fairbanks. They would have taken care of him," I said.

"Why keep him around?" asked Bob.

"For the same reason they keep any of us," said Sam; "it's cheaper than hiring new. Plus they had him for life now; he was never going to the Lower 48 with that kind of accident on his record."

"But how did they know he wouldn't do it again?" asked Bob.

"They would have known he learned something if he admitted it was his fault," said Scott.

"Said he was sorry?" asked Tony.

"Said something," said Scott, "said anything."

But Ray just kept sticking to it. He worked every day around the office doing anything the Company had for him, and all the time he refused, absolutely refused, to believe the maintenance reports on the airplane. He began to consider conspiracy theories about the Feds, which were entertaining for everyone to hear but quickly got more and more disturbing.

"We had all run the numbers by then, we had all talked to Maintenance, and we knew what the deal was with the plane," said Scott. "There wasn't a pilot at the Company who didn't like Ray, who didn't want the whole mess to be blamed on something else, but we knew the numbers and we knew there was no way he could have completed that flight the way he planned it."

"It was impossible," agreed Tony. "There was no way to land back in Nome without fueling along the way."

"Did anyone say anything to him?" I asked.

"He wasn't willing to listen," said Scott, shaking his head. "He made it clear that he wasn't going to listen to anyone who disagreed with him."

"So he didn't hear anything but his own story," said Bob.

"He didn't hear anything at all," said Scott.

The Feds came out with pilot error as the cause of the accident, and Ray's licenses were suspended for a year. By then no one was surprised, not even Ray. He talked to the Bosses and they needed him in the office, so it wasn't really that bad as punishment went. He would still be making money, and when his time was up he could get current again and go back on the line.

"It was going to be like it never happened," said Scott, "but that's the way it is sometimes. And Ray wasn't a bad guy, so no one wanted him to suffer. We all thought that maybe a year on the ground would make him change a little, that he'd rethink it and come around, admit he screwed up. Might even make him a better pilot."

"But he's not here, is he?" said Sam.

"No," said Scott, "he's not here."

At first Ray went to work and bitched about the Feds louder than anyone, but he seemed fine. He would go out sometimes by himself and walk around the airplane, even after the insurance company declared it a total loss and Maintenance started pulling off parts. No one understood why he stayed true to the lie, but there's a lot of weird shit that people do that no one understands. Ray went to work, and he did his job. Another ten months, then eight months, and he'd be flying again.

"But," I said.

"But he lost his fucking mind," said Tony.

"Yep," said Scott. "All of sudden, months after the crash, Ray just up and lost his mind."

For the longest time he hadn't dwelled on the accident, hadn't even thought about it except to wonder why it happened to him. Then one night, one night that wasn't the slightest bit different from any other, he had a dream. And the dream ended with all those girls screaming.

Out of the blue he just remembered it like it really happened. Maybe he had been so focused on the Feds, on trying to clear his name, that he hadn't really thought about the crash itself. Maybe he just blocked it all out. "Bottom line," said Scott "was that Ray never addressed what he did, never thought about it long and hard. He played the same kind of mind game on himself that he tried to play with everyone else. But the lie didn't stick, and finally, almost six months later, he started having dreams about it. When the girls started screaming and crying every night in his head, he realized he was having flashbacks."

"He was back in the cockpit?" asked Bob.

"Every night," nodded Scott. "He went back there every single night."

It wasn't the kind of thing that you talked about much, and Ray wasn't going to go see some doctor or anything. He figured it was normal maybe, a delayed reaction to the accident. Shit happens. And everyone knew the girls were fine. The rumor was the Company paid off the village to keep them from suing, so they were probably all running around on new four-wheelers; those girls were plenty fine out there.

So it wasn't a real concern Ray was having, or even a real guilt. It was just the truth finally coming out.

"You can't run and you can't hide," said Tony.

"Truth is gonna get you," laughed Bob ruefully.

"It got Ray good," said Scott. "It got him, and it wouldn't let him go."

"So he went crazy?" asked Sam.

"Mostly," said Scott, "he just went."

Maybe it was something in his childhood. We all knew that Bob's mother had fucked him up. And who the hell knew what made Casey like he was? So there had to be something that played a number on Ray. First it told him he was invincible, even when any fool could tell he was looking for trouble, then it told him he was innocent. Finally it turned into a monster and filled his head with late-night terrors he couldn't run away from. Whatever was going on with him, it wouldn't let him go, and he knew it was never going to.

"He told me that he made one of those girls pee her pants, she was so scared," said Scott. "He had them back there on the way down all begging God to let them live, promising to be good girls forever, promising to change their lives to however He wanted if He would help their pilot get the plane over the water. And he let them believe afterwards that he was a hero, that he was great. He stood there while they hugged him and held him and took all their grateful kisses. He told me all kinds of shit about that flight," said Scott, "like he had no choice, like he couldn't keep it in. And then he said he wasn't going to fly ever again."

"Even after he got his tickets back?" asked Sam.

"What tickets?" asked Scott. "He talked to the Feds about them, but he never tried to fly again. He said he didn't trust himself, couldn't trust himself. He couldn't get it all out of his head."

"It was supposed to make him a better pilot," said Bob, "when he finally acknowledged his mistake."

"Weird, isn't it?" said Scott. "It didn't even make him a better man."

And then Ray left. He was still working steady for the Company, mostly dispatching out in the Bush. He worked Bethel and Barrow and a few smaller villages. He didn't go back to Nome. He wasn't drinking or all of a sudden popping pills. He was coping with it, handling it. He just didn't want to fly anymore, and the Bosses were okay with that. No one was trying to push him.

"But Ray knew something they didn't know," said Scott, "that no one could know unless they had been there. He knew that you can't just lose your nerve like he did and still be okay. It doesn't work."

"You have to get back on the bicycle, or the horse, or whatever the fuck you fell off," said Tony.

"Whatever it takes," agreed Scott. "But Ray wouldn't fly any airplane, not cargo only, not even just by himself for fun. He wouldn't fly a damn thing."

"And then he left Alaska?" asked Bob.

"He left the whole world," said Scott.

———·—

No one knows what happened to Ray Marrs. Scott heard he was down in the Lower 48, throwing cargo for some airline somewhere. It was a like a Bigfoot sighting though, all rumors and not much else. His own family didn't even know where to find him. He just got on an Alaska Airlines jet and left Fairbanks one day. Maybe he thought distance was the answer, the way to make it all go away. Maybe he just didn't want to be in a place where anyone had ever heard of Nome, let alone Ray Marrs. Maybe he thought that would be the cure, that getting lost would fix him.

"You think he's still alive?" asked Bob.

"Who the fuck knows," said Scott.

"But what if he isn't? What if he killed himself?" asked Bob.

"Then we know that he died in Nome," said Tony.

"Never came back from the crash," agreed Scott. "We never saw him again."

"And that makes sense to you?" asked Bob. "That's enough?"

"No," said Scott, "but Ray didn't give us any choice here, did he? He fucked this story up from the very beginning, and now we'll never know. Nobody is ever going to know how it ends."

"Except Ray Marrs," I said.

"I don't think so," said Tony. "Ray knows less than anybody. He's still trying to figure out why he crashed, why he planned that flight in the first place. That's why he left. He couldn't stay here anymore, and he didn't know what else to do."

"He never knew what to do," said Scott. "Turns out, he never even knew how to fly."

And that's how the story ended, with no one knowing anything for sure about the life or death of Ray Marrs. He's throwing cargo somewhere, that's what we think. We've heard stories about him, and we believe them. He's throwing cargo somewhere.

Really.

He's throwing cargo, and he's thinking about flying again.

5

Flying Cold

Flying stories change with the audience; they become something that everyone will understand and accept. The important thing in the telling, though, is to keep the story literal; tell it like it was. This is flying after all, not love. There are not a thousand ways to do this and fewer ways to write it then you realize.

But remember your audience above all else.

———

After he left Alaska, Scott's Chalkyitsik story changed. He learned pretty quick that people could handle flying at thirty below, or even forty, but colder than that and they doubted flight was possible. They had vague suspicions about rubber splitting, hydraulic fluids turning solid, mysterious chemical reactions that could cause an aircraft to drop out of the sky. The Chalkyitsik story defied all of this and demanded more than a certain amount of trust in the storyteller. No one Outside wanted to believe Scott when he said it was common in Alaska to fly colder than forty below in prop-driven aircraft. They couldn't imagine it was just part of the job. The airline pilots he worked with called him a liar when he talked about Chalkyitsik, told him you couldn't do that kind of flying in a prop plane. So Scott stopped telling the story after a while, saving it instead for evenings when he was with his old friends.

The story always began in Fairbanks, where it was fifty-five below on the ground and no one was flying. The only reason Scott even showed up at the Company was to catch up on his paperwork and argue about a screwed-up pay-check. The other pilots were home, waiting for the weather to break or the airlines to get so desperate that they all started flying anyway. Scott didn't want to fly, didn't want to go to the trouble; but when the charter came up and the Bosses asked him if he would do it, he told them yes.

He still can't explain why he said that.

Ground temperature was only one factor in any flight, one small factor. All the other things were what might happen to the airplane—the threat of wear and tear on the flaps or the gear, the many other parts that you didn't want to suffer through too much movement in the cold air or on the frigid ground. Scott was flying 2KD, a twin-turbine Beech, to Chalkyitsik. He didn't plan to shut down either engine up there or adjust the flaps. All he had to do was take off, fly, and make a nice and easy landing for the sake of the struts. They would warm the plane up for a good long time before he left Fairbanks, so he knew it wouldn't be too miserable.

And Chalkyitsik was less than an hour in the Beech, an easy flight on any other day. Ops found a copilot and paid him double time to go along. So the two of them took off for the village, where it was already sixty-seven below.

When he used to tell the story Outside, this is where his listeners interrupted and asked him why. They expected to hear about a mercy flight, about saving lives. And he had to give them their first disappointment and admit it was only about the money. He was going up there to bring back the telephone guy, a tech who had flown out of Fairbanks the day before on a job at the school. But he didn't want to spend another night out there. The Company talked severe cold and hardship, and the Alascom guy offered double the standard charter rate. Just like that, the Owners decided it was perfect flying weather. And when they asked Scott he said sure, he could fly it.

Honestly, it was easy. Just the same cold he had been sleeping with for the past two years. And could you really tell the difference up there between thirty and fifty or forty and sixty? If you were going to fly into sixty-seven below, you just had to be ready to be cold and do your job anyway and worry about complaining later. This was a flight for a pilot who could get the job done and smile. And it was after he said yes, after he agreed to fly, that Scott realized the Owners asked him to go to Chalkyitsik because they knew he was a Company man.

He was the new Company man.

And when he had time to think about it later, he understood this was a more frightening revelation than anything that could happen in the flight. This new truth was downright terrifying the more he thought about it.

It was devastating.

But, still he flew to Chalkyitsik. Ops phoned ahead, and the agent had the passenger at the airport waiting with his gear when they got there. Scott landed without a problem, and the copilot popped open the door and got the guy in and everything stowed and locked up in less than three minutes. The whole flight was that way; over and done with pretty quick, and although the plane never got comfortable, everyone was bundled up enough to keep it bearable. It was okay; it was even uneventful. They got back to Town, the plane was fine, and the phone guy signed a big charge to the Alascom account. Scott was home three hours after he left, having a beer and watching cable with his dog. Another quiet night in the Young house; another night with nothing going on.

But what did it feel like? They had always asked him, the ones Outside, the ones who didn't fly. And Scott wondered why they would ask, how it wasn't all so fucking obvious. I flew to Chalkyitsik he told them; 1.8 hours block time, out and back. What did they think asking him those questions? Hadn't they heard any of the story? Didn't they understand what his job was?

It was like flying any other day, he said, like flying in June or July; it was just flying. It was cold, but it was always cold and no, he didn't worry about crashing because who the hell ever worried about that when they were flying? Temperature, like age, was just a number, a big number that day, an extreme number, but just a number for shock value more than anything else. It was like talking about the windchill in Bethel or Deadhorse; it was an adjective, that was all. It was just another way to tell the story, another way to show what it was like.

It wasn't supposed to be everything.

So he stopped talking about Chalkyitsik to people who couldn't understand it. He learned to give answers that said nothing when they asked what it was like to fly in the cold. Just flying, he would tell them, it's just like flying. Maybe he would tell them little things—that his coffee froze, that the new copilots always whined like babies, that the fur hat kept his head warm. Little things, easy things, things that meant nothing. They loved hearing them all.

And why try any harder? They would never understand anyway. Until you had been there and done it yourself, you were never going to understand.

But still, there was something about Chalkyitsik. It was the story that should have disappeared. If no one tells it then it dies, right? But that number was just too powerful to be ignored. Forget about what it felt like, all the emotional or psychological reasons behind the flight; the only reason we even still remember the whole thing is because of that damn number. No one at the Company ever flew colder when we were there; no one ever even tried. But the Chalkyitsik story is still about sixty-seven degrees below zero at destination and fifty-five below at departure point. That was straight temper-ature, no windchill, no wind at all. It was awesome cold, that was for sure; cold that almost went beyond the imagination. And we knew it; everybody on the ramp knew it.

So even when Scott didn't tell it, somehow the story kept going.

When anyone asked him about the cold, Scott could have told a hundred different stories. He could have talked about Fort Yukon at thirty below or Ruby at forty below or Barrow at fifty below. He could have talked windchill in Nuiqsut or Point Lay or Barter Island. He had a lot of experience freezing his ass off. He could pick any one of those stories; he could choose from literally hundreds of places and temperatures. He could have any story he wanted, but he couldn't help himself; he missed Chalkyitsik.

And damned if he could figure out why.

"I had nothing to prove," he said one night. "I'd already been there, done that. And the last people I have to show something to are the ones Outside. They wouldn't even understand what they were hearing anyway."

"So why go with Chalkyitsik?" asked Sam.

"Your shining moment," said Tony, shaking his head.

"You know better," said Scott. "It was my darkest hour."

"But nothing happened," I said. "It was a nonevent, just cold."

"Yeah. So what the hell was I doing out there? Didn't need the money, had a nice warm couch and cable TV waiting for me back at home. What was the point for me?"

"Company man," said Tony.

"Shit," said Sam, shaking his head, but agreeing.

"My darkest hour," repeated Scott. "So if I can't use it, if I can't make it a story about what it's like up here, about how it was for all of us everyday, then what the hell good is it? What was the point?"

"So what do you do with it?" I asked.

"Save it for parties and people who piss me off. It's a shock-value story; in your face, mother-fucker. No other value than that."

"And almost two grand to the Company," said Tony, who couldn't resist twisting the knife.

"Lucky day for them," agreed Sam.

"But you still don't know why you did it?" I asked. "Just said yes because the Owners asked you, no other reason?"

"Simple as that," said Scott; "just became a yes man somehow, picked it up like a habit."

"What you have to do is make the flight matter, make it important," said Sam.

"Salvage the story," agreed Tony, "make the sacrifice worthwhile."

"Save a life," I said. "You have to save a life."

"But there was no sacrifice," said Scott, "that was the point. It wasn't any big deal."

"Sold your soul to the Devil," said Sam. "Have to at least save someone's sorry ass in the process."

"Be a hero," said Tony. "It's the only way."

"And if I don't?" asked Scott. "If I don't change it?"

"Then it's the saddest story I ever heard," said Sam.

"A tearjerker," I agreed.

"Change it," said Tony, "and everyone will believe it. It's the story they want to hear anyway. The problem is that you're just not telling it right."

And that's what it's all about, isn't it? It's always about the story they want to hear.

I was there in the office that day, and I know for sure that it was sixty-seven below in Chalkyitsik because I was the one who checked. And Scott didn't have to take the flight. There was no reason for it, but what else is there to try and beat, after the fog and the snow and ceiling that comes down to the floor? What else can you do but fly in the cold? What else is there?

Now the whole truth, the truth even Scott can barely see, is that he took the flight because his marriage was a mess and his wife had just left him. Hell, he took it because they never should have gotten married in the first place. He took it because he didn't want to move to Alaska, because he longed to be a rock star and ended up a pilot, and because his father used to sit at the kitchen table and get drunk every night, telling his kids that no one understood or respected him, while his mother watched television and pretended not to hear. Scott took it because no one else wanted to. He took it because he always wanted to be somewhere else or, more importantly, someone else. He took it because they asked and he had no reason to say no. Back then, he had no reason for anything.

What the hell else was he going to do that day if he wasn't flying? What else was there?

I told him afterwards he should say he was rescuing a sick baby. Everybody loves the sick baby stories.

6

The Dead Body Contract

At one time or another, the Company hauled pretty much everything you could fit onto an airplane. Dead or alive, crated or loose, guns or food or mattresses, we crammed it in. The freight ranged from the loads we all hated (sled dogs) to the stuff we couldn't figure out (seven thousand pounds of candy for Fort Yukon one Christmas, which worked out to almost twelve pounds for each resident of the village) to the stuff we wished would just go away (cases of potato chips that weighed nothing but filled up the plane anyway). Nothing surprised us, not the crates of puppies or canoes. We adapted to the village way of life and travel because at the Company that was our way of life too. We were all living in the Bush when we worked at the Company; our addresses in Town were just geography and the least significant part of how we got the job done.

But then there was the Dead Body Contract.

My first lesson in death as freight was the body bag that leaked. The guy had been stabbed to death. The body bag had seen better days, and when the cargo guys pulled the body out of the plane in Fairbanks, there was a pool of blood and guts left behind on the floor. We all looked, we all saw it, but no one was going to clean that mess.

It wasn't in anyone's job description.

The cargo guys threatened to walk out if it was left to them, so finally the Bosses came out to the ramp and turned on the hoses and dealt with it themselves. We left the body in the shed while everyone argued about how to get him to Alaska Airlines without causing another mess in the Company van. We finally put cardboard down in the back and laid the body bag on top of it. Dealing with the leaking body pushed back the whole schedule, kept everyone from working, and was a total pain in the ass. I'm not sure anymore where the guy was from, or why he died. All I remember clearly is dealing with the mess. I didn't have time to feel sorry for the dead guy then; none of us did.

There was stabbed guy, drowned guy, Russian roulette with a shotgun guy. Guy hit by snow machine, guy who hit tree while on snow machine, lady shot to death, lady who drank to death, old man, older man, very very old lady. The guy who shot himself in the head and the next guy who did, and the next. Murdered at work, murdered at home, shot dead by cops because he shot first. Not one single wilderness death, no one done in by nature's savage beauty.

Just drive-by dying in the Bush because they were careless or bored or scared or sad or angry. Rolling four-wheelers, crashing trucks, sinking boats, and when there was nothing else, a rope and tree.

———·———

Bob Stevens had to deal with a hanging once, a weird sort of hanging. Bob was an okay guy, a little nervous, sometimes a little stressed, but he wasn't excitable; he wasn't the type to *panic*. He was just mostly confused, confused by how he ended up at the Company, ended up in Alaska, and ended up thirty-five years old without a wife or a kid or a mortgage. There were things that Bob expected from his life, and he couldn't figure out why they weren't happening. He was supposed to be happy at his age but wasn't, and he couldn't make sense out of that, so he couldn't make sense out of pretty much anything else either. That's why Bob was at the Company; he was waiting for his real life to find him and didn't have a fucking clue what he should be doing in the meantime.

Bob's hanging guy was in Allakaket, on a tree. He flew out on a charter with a state trooper to bring the body back. The trooper was pretty new on the job and young and female and fairly short. None of this mattered when she was staring at you over the barrel of a Glock 17, but when you have to catch a dangling body, it makes a big difference. It must have been obvious that she would be a problem in Fairbanks, but the troopers sent her out anyway, even though she was too small to reach the rope, even though she couldn't cut a body down.

Who do you think had to do it?

Bob didn't want to deal with it. "It was bullshit," he said later, "and the trooper knew it. I'm hired to fly the plane, and I know I have to help her load the body because it's freight and I have to load the freight, but when it is on a tree a mile from my airplane, then it isn't my freight and it isn't my problem. It was just bullshit, and she knew it."

But what could he do? Nobody else is around. The village cop disappeared right after he showed them the body, who turned out to be his cousin, and the trooper didn't want to wait on someone else. The dead guy had been out there since sometime the night before, and he was really starting to freak the locals out. Nothing good was going to come out of waiting. So it made sense to the cop to ask Bob to help her out a little, to cut the guy down. And that's how Bob became a guy who cut down the dead, a guy with somebody else's death smeared all over his hands. No way was this part of the real-life scenario he had been looking for, and he knew it. He knew right then that the white picket fence life he dreamed about was never gonna show up as long as he was doing that kind of shit for a living.

"I did it. I told her it was no problem and pretended like I did this shit every day. I stood on the same log the dead guy had kicked off from, and I reached up with my Leatherman and cut the rope. And when he fell I just stood up there on that log and watched him hit the ground. And the trooper stepped out of the way, actually moved away so that he had to hit the ground. Couldn't cut him down and wouldn't catch him either."

"That's a real professional," said Scott.

"No," said Bob, "that's a stone cold bitch. Watches the dead guy fall like a sack of potatoes. Like a bag of groceries, and she just watched him fall." He shook his head, "Just stepped aside and let him fall."

The two of them looked at the dead guy, and neither one of them wanted to pick him up. They didn't want to slide him into the body bag and load him on the bed of the borrowed truck and drive with him bouncing around back there out to the airplane. They didn't want to do it, but Bob stepped down and walked over and picked up the bag and the trooper helped him lay it out on the ground, and they lifted up the body together and he got it loaded on the truck and into the plane and the ride back to Town was no big deal, just a normal flight. And when she left him in Fairbanks, the trooper didn't say a word to Bob about the body; she just thanked him for a good flight. She had her paperwork and her report to fill out, and she walked away like she had done her job, like the mission was a success or something. And Bob went on his way into the hangar for his next flight trying to forget that sound, that nasty-ass sound of the body hitting the dirt and the way the trooper had looked right at him as she stepped out of the way. It was like she wasn't the slightest bit ashamed of the whole thing, like it was okay.

"Didn't want to get her hands dirty," said Scott, "that's the reason."

"And that makes it okay?" asked Bob. "She's new; maybe it's her first body and she doesn't know what the right thing to do is, the proper thing, but still it was wrong and she knew it."

"Guy was dead," said Scott. "What the hell did he care?"

"Better question is why the hell do I?" asked Bob. "Why the hell do I care?"

Here's the thing about Bob's story: It should have been a love story. If I had written it, Bob and the trooper would have hit it off in the air on the way out to Allakaket. Bob would have asked her out to dinner when they got back, and they would have sat out on the deck at Pike's until closing, talking like they had known each other forever. Years from now they would tell the story of how they first met at parties and holiday dinners, and no one would ever believe it. How could something so tragic and gruesome turn out to be so romantic? They would have lived happily ever after in my story. The Company could have used a few more of those.

We never found out why that guy hanged himself. To be honest, no one ever thought to ask.

———•———

Casey's dead body fell on the ground too. They were loading a casket into a single-engine, which meant they had to turn it sideways to get it in the door. Casey had the back end, and Cargo Bill was in the plane. They tilted the casket, Casey lost his grip, the lid popped open, and the body went tumbling out onto the ramp. It freaked Casey out so much that he dropped the casket and even screamed a little, although he denied that later. So Bill, a gold miner in the summers out in Nome and the toughest cargo guy ever, looks at Casey and tells him to put the old lady back. And Casey just starts shaking his head because how can that be his job, how can his job be loading some dead little old lady into a casket?

"She was just lying down there, stiff as a board and try-ing to be all dignified in the middle of the ramp," he said later. "I didn't know where I was supposed to put my hands, how we were going to put her back. And Bill wasn't help-ing. He was just waiting, like he was waiting for me to hand him a box or something. Like someone's grandma was just another box we had to make fit."

Bill wasn't going to move a muscle to help, no matter how long it took. If Casey could do the dropping, he could do the picking up. Bill said he'd sit there and wait all day if it took Casey that long to move her. They'd probably both still be out there if Tony hadn't taken pity and pushed Casey along, picking the lady up by the shoulders while Casey took her feet. He was laughing, though, laughing along with Bill. They were both laughing at Casey.

He was too busy trying not to throw up to care.

All of them dumped a body at one time or another; they actually got used to it after a while. Casket loads could be tricky; they were always taking everyone by surprise. Of course Bill and Shawn never dumped a body when they were loading, but they weren't in a hurry; they were careful. Pilots always wanted to get in the air right away though, and they rushed things. Bill and Shawn let them screw-up every now and again to teach patience, and to remind them that when it came to loading, most of them didn't know shit. (Bill and Shawn did however. They totally knew their loading shit.)

Tony dumped a body helping them unload a casket out of the Northern Air Cargo jet in Galena. Scott dumped one unloading in Arctic Village (getting them out of the single-engines was beyond tricky). Sam dumped one on the ramp in Fairbanks along with Bob, who was supposed to be holding up one end but got distracted and slipped on the ice. It happened often enough that everyone expected it, and no one felt bad about it because it was hard; it was awkward to load an adult-length casket into the door of one of those planes. And the families had to know that. They were out in the villages and helped with the unloading; they knew the score. Bodies were freight, and everybody understood that sometimes freight got dropped.

But still, the first time was hard.

Always though, if you had a choice, you wished for a casket, any casket over something else. There was the baby that died and came into Town in a duffle bag. The troopers didn't secure it when the plane took off, and the bag went rolling down the aisle until it hit the back wall. The copilot was so freaked out that he wouldn't fly after that; he wouldn't do anything but look out the window and try really hard not to keep hearing that sound the duffle made when it collided with the wall. The troopers laughed, but then nothing made those guys cry.

There was also the poor bastard who fell off his fishing boat and drowned in the Yukon. He wasn't found until two weeks later, and by then his body was so swollen that they couldn't fit him in a body bag and had to send him into Fairbanks with just a tarp as a cover. It slipped off during take-off, and Frank was all alone with the dead guy in the back who didn't have a face anymore. He popped open a beer in the parking lot when he got back after that flight—he would've started drinking in the plane if he could have gotten away with it.

We had one dead boy who had made a suicide pact with his four friends. They sat around a campfire, got wasted, and thought about all the reasons they had for not living past that night. Then one boy took the shotgun and blew himself away. We said later he must have scared the rest of them back into living, because the death was so real and so awful that none of the other boys followed through. They sat there for who knows how long, stunned by what they saw, by what was left of their buddy spread all over the place around them, and all those bad things that were killing them went away. The cold reality was that the kid died for the same reason so many do: Life was hard, and he didn't know why he kept trying to live it.

The first few times we brought in dead boys, I thought it was awful. When they came in after hanging or shooting or stabbing themselves or each other, I thought we should find out what happened; we should help them; we should try to save them The worst thing about working at the Company was that it made me understand there are bigger things to dying then anyone caring. It seemed like we weren't living in the same place or even the same century when they pulled those triggers. They were dying over something that happened two hundred years ago to an ancestor that never made it into a history book. They were dying from the past; it just took them into the present before they could finally do it.

At least that was how it seemed to me after a while, and I was the only one who really thought about it. The pilots flew the bodies and shook their heads but didn't dwell on the dead. Then again, they had to load those body bags; thinking about it wasn't going to make those flights any easier for anybody.

Johnny Cart was the son of one of our agents in a village north of Fairbanks, a nice kid who used to come into Town every now and again with his parents. He sometimes met the planes in the village, and all of us knew him and his sister and liked them both. We never heard a bad thing about Johnny, never had a hint of trouble or that he was looking for a reason to end it all. Then one night while his parents were watching TV, while his whole family was on the other side of the wall, he walked into his bedroom, picked up his gun, and blew himself away. Johnny was maybe sixteen when he died, and his mother fell into the kind of little pieces that never seem to go back together again.

That death made us all pause, made us think about the last time we saw him, the day before when we talked to his father, the last few words anyone exchanged with that kid at the airport. Was Johnny different somehow in the last week? Was he sad or distracted or confused? Where were all those warning signs you hear about? Did his parents know something? Did Johnny even know it was coming?

His mother found God, and He showed her the way to go on living. That was what she told me the next time she came to Town. Johnny was in a better place now, she said, and we agreed because what else could we do? Maybe God was right; maybe anyplace was better than the end of the world he was living in.

But thinking about it that way, wrapping my head around Johnny's choice to take a chance on an unknown afterlife over another day at home made me realize that he and I were more alike than I was comfortable with. He just was running away too, except where he came from it wasn't so easy to go off to college or catch a big plane looking for adventure. In his world you got a gun and let it take you away because all the necessary planning and waiting and *hoping* for a different future was too damn hard. The gun was instant; the gun was best. And as frustrating as it was to see all those boys die over and over again, I could understand that longing to run away forever. For them the gun wasn't a bad thing; it was a golden ticket out of everything that broke their hearts. As wrong as it was, the gun was how Johnny and the other dead boys got to fly away.

That's why this will always be the saddest flying story I ever heard.

———

But then there was this.

When Henry Smoke passed away in the hospital, his family asked the Company to send Tony home with the body. They wanted a pilot who knew Henry and could call him by name. Tony had been flying in and out of the Upper Yukon for years, and Henry was the Company's agent in Stevens Village forever. The two of them went way back. When Tony landed in the Navajo, most of the folks from Stevens and the surrounding villages were on the ramp waiting for the plane. They unloaded the heavy, ornate casket, placed Henry down in the back of a waiting truck, and then drove slowly away. Tony waited until he was the only one left at the airport before he started up the engines. He said later he wanted to preserve the quiet for as long as possible—he wanted to keep the ground *holy.*

Tony was not a religious man, but there you go. For Henry Smoke, that was the word he thought of.

He said later he was glad he took that flight, that they asked for him. He packed Henry's flight away with the ones to keep with him, and when Tony left Alaska he had well over ten thousand hours of flight time, but Henry Smoke was the only body he knew by name.

7

Finding the Walls of a Box Canyon

This is how you fly into a mountain on a clear day. You fly low because you're bored. You have a load of cargo, just a bunch of tri-packs of pop going to some improbably small village that you never heard of until you started living in Kotzebue. You fly low and you look for wolves, because that is the game everyone at the job has been playing for the last week. There's a wolf pack out there, and if you get down around fifty feet, you can really make them run. You can chase the pack across the tundra and it is so freaking *National Geographic*—so right out of one of those wildlife shows that you never thought was real that you can't believe it. And even though you know you should be flying the straight shot, you should be doing your job and getting back fast so that you can get on to the next load, you can't resist going after those wolves. They are so damn cool and so purely what you never dared hope you would find up here that you just keep thinking a little bit farther, a little bit farther and then I'll get back to the job, then I'll get back to doing what they pay me to do.

But all that time you've been flying along, all that time you've been so low, you've made some turns that brought you to a place you've never been. You look up, you look around, and you see for the first time that you don't know where you are—that you are lost in a spot on the map that no one knows is there, that no one ever cared enough to find.

And then there is no way out of the place you have found yourself in.

There are box canyons all over Alaska; in every mountain range there are places to draw you in that will not let you out. Being smart means staying high, learning the land, finding out what's good and bad about every route, every destination. It means not getting down to treetop level when you don't have room to get back up.

Being smart means living to fly another day and not getting lost when there's nothing but mountains all around you and no time left to clear the tops.

My friend Luke flew into a mountain.

———·———

I knew about Luke's crash only hours after it happened. In a lot of ways he was just another one of those twenty-something guys who came to Alaska looking for flight time and adventure, but for me he was much more; he was someone I *knew*—someone from before, from Outside, from home.

When he showed up to fly for the Company I thought Luke had a decent shot, but he was low on flight time and barely met the minimums to be hired as a copilot. Everyone knew he must have pencil-whipped the numbers; there was no way they all could be true. But he was friendly and eager and determined to get a job, any job that would see him flying. And everyone liked him at the Company; Luke was so easy to like.

The only problem was that Luke thought he had a job waiting for him when he got to Fairbanks and was maybe just a little bit too cocky that way—too sure of everything. That was the only thing the Bosses really did not like in a pilot. They didn't like arrogance until you had earned the right to it—until you had proven you had a place or, more importantly, until everyone else decided you were good.

They didn't like copilots who thought they were as good as captains.

The days dragged on for him with no one making a decision, and Luke got antsy, got tired of sleeping on someone else's couch while he waited for a paycheck. So he took his résumé and his buffed-up logbook and he made phone calls and he got a job in the Bush. He got hired by a commuter flying single-engines out of Kotzebue in the middle of fucking nowhere. And he told everyone, his old friends and his new ones, that this was the best thing he could do. This is where he would learn what it was really like to fly in Alaska; this would be more real than anything he could do flying out of Fairbanks. This was the kind of job you were supposed to come to Alaska for.

Luke laughed heading out the door as he told the Bosses he would be back; he would see us in a few months, maybe a year, and he would have the flight time and experience that would make him an easy hire. It was the best thing he could do for his career, he said. All he had to do was be smart and he would be back; that was all he had to do. How hard is that?

On a good weather day—on a CAVU afternoon where the sky was crystal clear and the visibility went on forever— Luke took off from Kotz in a perfectly good airplane and ended up on the backside of a mountain. He was close to making it—just fifty feet low according to the Feds who went over the wreckage, maybe even less. He was trying to climb out of that canyon, but he didn't have enough, not enough power and not enough time. He hit the mountain and he flipped the plane and he rolled over the peak and then he burned; everything burned. By the time the plane stopped rolling, everything was burning. The mountain was on fire, and Luke was far away and gone.

No one ever saw that wolf pack again.

Because I knew him, because he was not just a friend but a friend from before, a friend from beaches and keg parties and shorts and T-shirts, I thought there should be someone to blame. Luke had no mountain flying experience. Wasn't that something his company should have taught him when he was first hired? Shouldn't his company have sent him out with an experienced pilot for some hours flying around the area? Shouldn't someone have flown with him in those canyons or brought him along on some flights through them or at least talked to him about the mountains? Isn't that something they should have to do; that they would want to do?

In those few months he was with them, shouldn't they have done something that might have saved him?

That's what I want now, what I have wanted from the first phone call about Luke's accident: a way to blame someone else. I want to know that it was all someone else's decision, that there was pressure or threats or fear of losing his job. I want this accident to be about something other than Luke because it needs to be; it needs to be about someone else or it's just Luke and some wolves and that mountain, and that leaves me with nothing. That leaves me with just my friend making a stupid, and utterly preventable, mistake.

There are no rules for protecting pilots from themselves. The mountains are always going to be out there, and everybody knows it. Just don't fly into them and you will be fine. Take the load, get there, get back, and go out again. That's what flying in Alaska is all about, and it's hard. Everyone knows it is hard, but that's on the bad weather days, on the days of wind and snow and ice and cold. That's when going out and coming back is harder than anyone can imagine when they still live someplace else; that's when it gets close to impossible.

That's when you have an excuse.

"Can't save a pilot from hitting a mountain if that's what he's going to do," said the Fed to me after the accident. "Can't save someone from themselves." And he looked at me hard so that I would get the message, I would understand. I would see what the truth really was about Luke's accident and forget the story I wanted to hear.

I knew that, but still. That day at the Company, that day he was so proud of his new job in Kotzebue, so proud that someone wanted *him,* I saw Luke at the end of the hallway and I saw the Bosses and I knew that I could stop it. They listened to me; sometimes they listened to me a lot, and I knew that if I pulled them aside and said he was the one we needed right now, that he might be a little cocky but that wasn't so hard to fix and wasn't cocky better than timid anyway? Didn't you want a guy who was ready to go instead of one who was always looking for excuses? It was so much easier for us to stop them, to make them wait, than it was to push them out the door.

So much easier for us to say no than to make them say yes.

I thought about all these things that day, and I thought about him staying and learning with us, but I didn't say anything, didn't do anything. Because before Luke crashed I still believed in the Bush; I still thought it made pilots stronger, better. It made them more willing to fly when I needed them to fly, when I wanted them to get the job done. Flying in the Bush made them grateful to fly in Town, and grateful made my job easier.

I thought if he went to Kotzebue and came back with that kind of flight time, it would make my job easier. And back then, that was all I really cared about.

So I stood at one end of the hallway in that piece-of-shit building where we all made our hard living, and I watched him and I decided to let him go. I wished Luke well, and I made the same jokes as everyone else. I told him he would be a tough guy when I saw him next; he would be a for-sure-honest-to-God badass.

I told him he would be a good pilot and then I would have trouble telling him what to do, and he laughed at that because he knew I'd try anyway. He knew I would still be on him when he came back and that was okay, because then he would be able to push right back like the other guys, like the captains, like the ones who had earned it.

Like the real Alaskan pilots.

And so I watched him go. I believed when he left that the Bush was the best place for pilots to learn about flying and the place for Luke to be. I believed everything I had heard and read about flying in Alaska back then; I believed it all.

Luke's crash was my first lesson in what I didn't know. He was my first hard truth and the story I never wanted to hear.

For the longest time, for years after the accident, I blamed Luke's company for killing him. They did this, I thought, they let this happen. They all should have known better than to tell a new guy about the wolves; to make chasing them into a game that sounded only about fun and never about danger.

They should have seen what might happen.

That was my argument every time Luke's crash came up: He was too young, too inexperienced, too eager to believe he could live forever. And then one day, years later and long after both of us left Alaska, Scott told me how wrong I was about the accident and everything else about Luke and flying.

"He would have crashed flying for us just as easy as he did flying for them," he said. "You don't want to see that—you've never wanted to see that—but it was obvious to everyone who talked to him that he was going to take chances. It wasn't the wolves that brought Luke down," he said. "The only reason he saw those wolves in the first place was because he was flying so damn low *looking for something to chase.*"

And that was it. Maybe he wouldn't have crashed at the Company because maybe we never would have given him that chance. But it is just as likely he would have found another mountain, another reason to be in the wrong place at the wrong altitude.

"He flew into a mountain," said Scott. "You can't save someone who's going to fly into a mountain."

And I know that; I always knew that. But there is still what I didn't say in that hallway so long ago. It's stupid; it's pointless and it probably wouldn't have mattered, but still. I can't resist the wish that if only I had done something different then this would not be a story about a dead pilot who was my friend. This wouldn't be a story at all.

I don't want Scott's truth because that's where Luke would have missed the crash in Kotzebue but would have found a mountain outside Dillingham or Nome or Anaktuvuk. He would have found his different time and different place, because it was always waiting for him.

You can have a thousand "if onlys," and not one of them will make a difference when you fly stupid; nothing will ever make a difference. The wolves are always going to be running somewhere, and if you're determined to chase them, then nothing and no one is going to save you.

———•———

How do you fly into a mountain on a perfectly clear day? You don't see it, that's how. You look everywhere but where you should be looking; you see everything but what you should be seeing; you do everything but what you should be doing.

You fail to see that fucking mountain.

You don't fly the airplane like a commercial pilot; you fly it like a student or a child or a fool. You fly it like someone who thinks he is lucky to be in Alaska, someone excited to be out there in the wilderness, like a tourist seeing wolves for the very first time.

You never think to look for it, and so you fly right into a mountain that you didn't know was there.

And within a week, your company hires someone else to take your place, and he doesn't know a damn thing about mountains either.

Welcome to the Last Frontier.

8

On the Other Side of the Mountains

In the summer of 2007 I spent a week sitting in front of a microfilm reader on the third floor of the Rasmuson Library at the University of Alaska at Fairbanks. For part of that time I was researching Russ Merrill and Noel Wien's attempt to reach Barrow on a tandem charter flight in 1928. The floor was empty every afternoon as I pulled the rolls of film from back issues of the *Fairbanks Daily News-Miner,* looking for articles that tracked the increasing concern for the two pilots who were lost with their three passengers.

Wien Alaska Airways was hired by Fox Films that May in 1928 to charter two aircraft up to Barrow, where the filmmakers planned to record scenes of "Eskimo life." Noel Wien offered Merrill, who operated Anchorage Air Transport, half the work. At this time the Arctic slope was unsurveyed, and maps reflected only the larger mountain ranges and rivers. Neither of the pilots had flown in the region before.

Wien and Merrill decided to fly with wheels rather than skis, as the runway in Fairbanks was dry and it was anticipated that Barrow would be as well. They took off on May 13 with heavy loads and flew through the mountain passes because they couldn't climb up high enough to clear the peaks. Two hundred miles out of town they stopped in the gold mining camp of Wiseman and refueled. From there a radio message was sent to Fairbanks confirming their departure. This was the last message received for weeks.

Four and half hours out of the camp, north of the Endicott Mountains and after crossing what they believed was the Colville River, they ran into a bank of solid fog. With no other options, the two pilots landed on a frozen lake to wait out the weather.

The next morning Wien's aircraft, which had larger tires, was able to take off, but Merrill's was not. Wien lightened his cargo and took one passenger, planning to fly on to Barrow and return with skis for Merrill. He did make it to the village that day, but a strong wind and blowing snow obscured the route he had flown and he could not locate Merrill's plane again when he tried to return. Then a blizzard blew in and forced Wien to stay on the ground in Barrow. It raged for six days and there was nothing he could do; there was nothing anyone could do. Russ Merrill and his two passengers were left to try to survive on their own.

It was eighty degrees as I scanned the pages telling the saga of the missing men. Sitting in the artificial coldness and quiet of the belowground Alaska Collection of the library, I read every article from every state newspaper dated May, June, or July 1928 about Wien and Merrill. The story shifted quickly from one of anticipated triumph: "Start Sunday on a Second Commercial Flight to Be Made to Continent's Tip" to the all-too-common uncertainty of "No Word Received [*sic*] Overdue Aviators." Ralph Wien ramped up to get the job done in his brother's absence and set off for Nome with the mail that had to be delivered to fulfill the territorial contract. Two main stories ran then through the front page in the days that followed his departure: one Wien missing and possibly dead while another flew in the opposite direction to get the job done.

The biggest drama in the lives of two families played out as the pages glided by on the reader, but the only sound on the entire library floor, where I was always completely alone, came when I hit the print button to collect a copy. Everyone I was reading about was dead—Ralph Wien and Russ Merrill in 1929, Noel Wien decades later. Barrow resident Charlie Brower, who organized the search from Barrow, asking Noel for every recollection he had of a mountain or river that might aid them, died in 1945.

Everyone who knew this search as something that mattered was long gone.

The town's collective fear and concern that summer was a history so dusty I had to search it out in newspapers that no one else was reading. This was a flight where no one died, no place was explored, and no discoveries were made. In those ways it was more like the Company than anything else. The world didn't change because of the 1928 Barrow flight, and it didn't change because of what we did every day either. The only thing transformed on the Wien-Merrill flight was an understanding of the northern landscape shared by a handful of pilots. Back then that was a lot though; for Alaska aviation, knowing the ground beneath you was life and death and more. The lessons learned in the 1928 Barrow flight were about when you couldn't find your way or, worse, when you couldn't find your way back.

Sometimes that still happens in Alaska.

When they arrived in Barrow, Noel Wien and his passenger were confident of where they had left Merrill and the others. They told Charlie Brower they had traveled about one hundred miles from the frozen lake where Merrill's aircraft was stranded. From their recollection, they had flown north after takeoff and then, after seeing "a herd of deer near the coast," had followed the coastline west until they started seeing houses. That was how they found Barrow. They thought it would be easy enough to relocate the reindeer camp and then fly south until they hit the lake. Brower was skeptical, and after two days of trying the men had to admit that the snow and fog had masked the landmarks they were so certain of; or perhaps their own confident memory of what they had seen was actually far off the mark.

Brower, a white man born in New York City and a successful whaler who had lived in Barrow for forty years when Wien arrived, recounted his early conversation with the two men in his memoir, *Fifty Years Below Zero:*

> *Were they sure it hadn't taken longer to reach the deer camp than they had thought when they first came out? And how about the wind? That would make a difference too.*

From what they said now it seemed to me that the lost plane might be farther south than they had estimated; perhaps even south of the Tashicpuk River and near the Colville.

Wien had never been to Barrow before, and while Brower and the other residents of the village had not seen the area from the air, they did have a relationship with the region that the pilot could not approach. More importantly, they were able to remind him how easily everything could change in the north and how foolish it was to ever be confident when it came to country covered in snow. This was particularly true of a place where every mountain was foreign to Wien; where every dip in the landscape was just one more chance to forget where he had been.

Brower organized six dog teams, which left on May 23 for the deer camp and points south. That day Noel Wien also left to search again, and a few hours later a new pilot, Matt Nieminen, arrived from Fairbanks. It had taken this long for a relief aircraft to arrive there from Anchorage and launch north seeking word on the missing men.

Nieminen arrived just in time to begin multiple searches for Wien, who vanished for a week in the fog. When Wien did return it was with news from Cape Halkett, about 120 miles to the east, where he had waited out the weather. (It was after this latest miracle that Brower wrote he resolved to ". . . never again worry about *anything*.") Wien had met a Native hunter who reported seeing two planes several weeks earlier when he was camping at an area far to the south. After talking to him, Wien realized he had indeed gotten off track in his search and Brower was correct; Merrill's plane was farther south then he originally thought. There was another wait for the weather to break, but now, with the hunter's camp as a guide, they had an idea of where to aim. On June 2 both pilots departed, and a few hours later Nieminen sighted Merrill's plane.

None of this was reported in the newspapers I was reading though. The editors only knew that not only were Wien and Merrill overdue but now so were Nieminen and his passenger, who had taken a wireless along and planned to update the city on the search. As Brower recorded, they were unable to do this because of broken equipment. The people of Fairbanks saw more pilots fly north and disappear, and the tone of the articles became increasingly desperate.

"With another day gone by without word of the seven flyers who are missing somewhere in the Arctic," reported the *News-Miner* on June 2, "the persons in Fairbanks most intimately connected with the flights feel the need for a second relief expedition to be imperative and are doing everything in their power to make arrangements for the sending of another plane north." The headline read: "Relief Measures for Lost Flyers Are Urged Here."

For the searchers, discovering Merrill's plane yielded clues but no survivors. From his carefully maintained log, the rescuers learned that at first the three men stayed with the plane, but on May 19, after the weather cleared, Merrill's two passengers set out on their own. The group was nearly out of supplies, and they knew they had no choice but to try to walk to Barrow. The men all thought it was only about sixty miles north to the village, a miscalculation of their location similar to Wien's. Nieminen immediately flew north per the notes in the log. A few hours later he found the passengers; one of the men had lost thirty pounds and the other forty, but they were alive. Russ Merrill, unfortunately, was not with them.

Two days after his passengers left, Merrill had tried to take off again but damaged the plane in this attempt and was left with no alternative but to walk out also. He left his logbook behind with a note and directions on where he was headed. The last words he wrote were "Dearest love to my wife, boys and two fine brothers. R. H. Merrill." And then, on May 24, he started walking north.

After finding his passengers, the search for Merrill kicked into high gear. He was finally found on June 4, forty miles from Barrow, by a dogsled team led by trapper John Hegness of Halket Station. By then Merrill had shot, killed, and eaten raw lemming to stay alive and, overcome with exhaustion, was lying down in the snow. Although he initially appeared to be in excellent health at Barrow, over the next few days and weeks he became very ill. Because of his increasingly weak condition, it was almost two months later, on July 26, before he made it home to Anchorage. He was later believed to have contracted Rocky Mountain spotted fever during his ordeal.

Writing about the flight thirty years later, Ada Wien still remembered the uncertainty she suffered until she received word that her husband was alive:

For three and one-half weeks we had no news of them. In Alaska three and one-half weeks usually seems as fleeting as a moment, but this particular three and

one-half weeks seemed endless to some of us. There was
so little anyone could do.

It was Thyra Merrill I thought about the most though. She is rarely mentioned in the news reports, but the pages of the book her son later wrote about his father's career reveal much of what she went through in those months. Thyra rushed to Fairbanks, he wrote, and ". . . steeled herself for the shock of seeing him after his two months of suffering." Nothing could have prepared her, however, for the change in her husband, so ". . . strong and healthy when he left Anchorage in mid-May," but now he ". . . looked old and frail." Still, he was alive. "When she saw the life that still shone in his eyes, she knew he would be fine."

Thyra was wrong on that score unfortunately. Russ Merrill disappeared forever on September 16, 1929, on a flight between Anchorage and the New York–Alaska Company mine at Nyac, near Bethel. He planned to stop en route at Sleetmute, on the Kuskokwim River, that night. As Robert Merrill MacLean later wrote in his book, his father was also ". . . planning to briefly head south down Cook Inlet before turning west toward the mine." He never made Sleetmute.

All the weeks of waiting and searching did not bring him home this time. "Search Fails to Locate Plane of Missing Aviator," read the headlines. In 1928 Thyra Merrill was lucky; one year later her aviation dream was over. With both Merrill and Eielson dead, the Alaska aviation fairy tale ended and everyone learned that sometimes, what you hope for just doesn't stand a chance of coming true.

———•———

Standing on the ramp in front of the Company hangar looking toward the White Mountains, all you can see are the hills north of Town. The morning ritual—after the downriver flights were gone but the nine o'clock flight to Fort Yukon was still waiting—included walking outside to see if the hills were clear. Talking over cigarettes, coffee, and my first jolt of iced tea, we had discussions about whether going north to take a look was worth it. There is a whole different class of weather reporting in Alaska now from the dark days of the late 1920s, but it's still not nearly as technologically advanced as it should be. On days of snow and fog, I had to call the village agents and ask them how it looked on the ground—if it was clear across the river, if the hills were open, if they could even see out their window. The Bosses smoked, the cargo guys waited for a decision, and collectively we looked north. We all wanted to know what could happen up there, if the plane could get in or would have to turn back: if it was worth it to try; if it was pointless to launch.

Mostly, though, we wanted to send a flight that we knew could get where it was going. The pilots had their own opinions, which varied from extremes of supreme confidence (they could get in no matter the weather) to absolute uncertainty (they could only guarantee getting in if it was clear) and even complete paranoia (if they were being asked to do anything illegal then they were not going to fly, so they needed to know for sure it was going to be legal from start to finish before agreeing to take the flight).

But standing out there looking at the hills was no way to know for sure that a flight would be successful, just like calling the agents didn't guarantee that nor did sending out the most determined pilot. It was habit that sent us outside more than anything, and we went there nearly every day to make the same observations: It was clear or it wasn't; it was snowing or it wasn't; it was foggy or it wasn't. The flight might make it in or it wouldn't.

Nature isn't going to tell you anything about flying in Alaska, except when it's a very bad idea. (Something Mount McKinley pilot Don Sheldon knew better than anybody.) But everyone always wants to take a look; they want to stand on their front porch and see what the sky will tell them, and they want to take off and climb and see if the horizon will reveal a secret. On a bad weather day, getting in or not is mostly just a crapshoot; that and the difference between pilots who know what the fog is hiding and those who never took the time to learn what the ground looked like when it was good.

Tony flew the downriver run so often that he could get into Nulato with less than a mile visibility. "You fly down the south side of the river," he would say, "and make your turn for right base where there was this one specific old tree. It wasn't dead but it was almost dead, and it stood out from the others; I knew that tree. Once I could make the turn, then I flew on from there a few more seconds until I caught the bank on the right side of the river and turned for final. It was easy when you knew what to watch for."

You have to know every lake, every stream, every bog, every bend in the river and the trees around the village and near the runway. The turn in Beaver Creek was marked by "Big Rock," and knowing that specific rock from all the others near and far from it could get you into Fort Yukon.

Joe Robinson was a pilot with the competition who crashed because he didn't know the distance from Bettles to the end of the Brooks Range. On a crap day he let down too early and flew right into the side of a mountain—the last mountain between him and home. He should have known to stay high until he was clear of that mountain; he should have known that range like his hometown, like his neighborhood, like his backyard.

Everywhere, you have to know everywhere. "I can get in," one of the pilots would tell us, looking at the fog obscuring the hills. If he was someone who knew the ground, then we let him go and do it one more time.

———•———

Don Sheldon knew Mount McKinley like no other pilot before him; Bob Reeves claimed the routes in the Aleutians so well that the military asked him for help during World War II. Noel Wien, Ben Eielson, and Harold Gillam flew the Interior memorizing sloughs and dogsled trails, and Russ Merrill even had a pass named for him across the Alaska Range after he established it as a shortcut to and from the Y-K Delta. First they flew blind, and then they learned, and then they knew and to a certain degree; that hasn't changed.

"I can get downriver at less than a mile any day of the week," said Tony, and he was right. He didn't need good weather to fly. He just needed to go in the direction he knew, to the place that was as familiar as his own house, on a route that lived in his memory better than any map.

Landscape will change though, and it is at its most fluid where people live. Cape Halket, home to the native hunter who recalled seeing Merrill and Wien's aircraft and the trapper who rescued Russ Merrill, was completely unknown to us at the Company. Charlie Brower mentions it several times in his book, and traffic between Halket and Barrow was common in his day. It was used as a whaling station in the late nineteenth century and then as a camp for a time after the whaling dried up in the 1920s. But beyond its name still being on the navigation charts, I had to look in history books to discover why Halket had ever mattered. For all intents and purposes, it has vanished, ceding its significance to other places. Flying the North Slope doesn't mean looking for Halket anymore; now those routes are all about other places, other names, other personal landmarks.

The maps can't tell you the places you have to know, the ones that matter. That's what you discover on your own, flying on the good days and paying attention. If you're smart, you build your own map in Alaska. You build your own map—and you never forget it.

9
Mercy Flight

There's some shit I couldn't make up, not even if I tried. Every time I thought I knew what to expect at the Company, I was reminded all over again how crazy an idea that was. It was the stories that made the least amount of sense that really stayed with me though; the ones that came from so far out in left field that we couldn't see them until they landed; the ones that taught us all how foolish it was to ever think we knew what was going on or, even more so, what would happen next.

Amber Durrell was a beautiful girl, but Tony never noticed. When he saw her she was laid out on a stretcher, IVs running into both arms, an oxygen mask covering most of her face. As far as he knew she was dying, and there was no reason to doubt it. From the first moment the PA came into the office in Galena, rushing around, telling everyone to hurry up, to get the plane back in the air, to get to

Fairbanks as soon as possible, it had all been about Amber Durrell dying.

"You had to hear her mother to believe it," he said later, "wailing and screaming the whole time, more like an animal than a person, like something caught in a trap somewhere, screaming for its life, begging for some kind of release. I listened to that for an hour and half, that woman's crazy screaming."

She never stopped.

And the whole time Tony was flying, the PA was pumping Amber full of drugs, yelling over the engines at the Ruby Health Aide to get him everything he needed before he needed it, and the girl just kept lying on that board, her eyes rolled back in her head and not saying anything. She wasn't even looking like she was going to live.

Amber Durrell was dying, and Tony was the only chance she had to get to Town and live.

If he had been a regular medevac pilot, if it was his job every day to fly the desperate and dying, then maybe Tony would have been more prepared for what the whole thing could look like. But when we were with the Company, there were no regular medevac operations in the Interior. There was just the unwritten rule that the closest plane had to take the patient. You had to get rid of your passengers, dump the mail and the freight, and take the patient. You made it work. And the Company loved it; every airline loved it when someone got sick. I mean you felt sorry for the family (of course, of course), but medevacs were big bucks and great publicity, so you took them, no question. They were a gold mine. You hopped at the chance for a medevac.

Tony was lucky to get Amber Durrell offered to him on her stretcher, all gray and green and dying, and he knew it. Everyone but Amber knew he was lucky.

When it happened, Tony was in Galena with a plane-load of passengers, picking up some mail, getting bags all sorted out, and giving everyone the five-minute warning to head to Town. Then the clinic PA came charging into the office yelling that he needed the plane, he's taking the plane; he has a patient in Ruby, and she is for sure dying if they don't get her to Town. Tony had the only twin-engine on the ground in Galena, so he was the one who had to go. And just like that he had no choice; just like that he was saving someone's life. He was going to be a hero whether he wanted to or not.

So all bets were off, all the rules were changed. A life-or-death flight means the pilot does whatever he can do. *Whatever he can do.* Knowing this, Tony does what any other pilot in Alaska would do and says yeah, he'll take the flight; he'll get the girl. He will save her life. He tells the passengers, the Bosses get a phone call, and everyone starts to do what they have to, with the whole schedule suddenly thrown up in the air. But it's working; it's going to work. All he has to do is unload the plane, yank the seats, and leave with the PA to get the girl. And then the fucking nuns refuse to give up their seats.

I'm going to write that again: The fucking nuns refuse to give up their seats.

Here's the deal: When you put a patient on a Piper Navajo on a stretcher, that means you have to yank all the seats out of the back and the aisle is going to be blocked. If the aisle isn't open, then the Feds say no paying passengers; it's a black-and-white safety reg. But the nuns don't care. They were just out in the Bush for two weeks at the mission in Kaltag, and that was it. They aren't local, and they aren't willing to wait; and even though they don't want anyone to die, they aren't going to give up their paying seats for some village girl who didn't make a reservation. They have a connecting flight out of Fairbanks to make, plans to go back to the Lower 48 that cannot be changed. They have made arrangements. And even though this might be an act of God, they are still pretty sure that the dear Lord would not want them to be stuck in Galena.

So they refuse to give up their seats. And Tony tells them they can't do that; they can't refuse because he is the captain, and he is telling them to stay off his plane. And they tell him they are flying to Fairbanks, now. And so there they are, the three of them, fighting over seats. And Tony wants to go, but they won't stay out of his face, and the PA is coming to pieces while the cargo guys are offloading the plane, and the nuns walk out on the ramp and get in the middle of everything, get in the way. And with their crosses and their Bibles, they refuse to give up their seats.

"It's was surreal," said Tony.

"It was something," said Scott, "that's for sure."

"They really just wouldn't let you go; they were going to block the plane or something?" asked Casey.

"No, they weren't getting all protest march or anything. They were just standing there, in the way, refusing to listen to reason. They just kept making it hard—my job, the PA's, the rampers'. Everyone's jobs. They wouldn't let us do what we had to do."

"So you gave them their seats," said Scott. "You gave in to the Jesus freaks."

"I didn't do anything. The Company did. Bosses said since seats 3 and 4 don't come out anyway, let the nuns fly."

"You're blocking the aisle with the stretcher out of Ruby," said Scott.

"Blocking it all the way back to Town," agreed Tony.

"For a couple of nuns who don't give a shit about anything but their connecting flight," I said.

"Yeah."

"But you did it anyway."

"Stupid fucking nuns," said Tony.

"But still," repeated Scott, "you did it anyway."

"Yeah," said Tony, "I did it anyway."

———•———

It was a twenty-minute flight to Ruby, and when they got there the agent had Amber and her mother and the health aide waiting. It was clear to everyone the girl was in serious trouble. They got her on the plane as fast as they could, and Tony had them in the air as soon as the stretcher was strapped down. It was five minutes, maybe ten before he realized it was going to be a really shitty flight home. There was a low overcast that wasn't moving and serious headwinds at altitude. He was going to be fighting the clouds all the way and have to go low to make it a fast trip. And it had to be a fast trip. He was going to have to scud-run with this crazy woman screaming in the seat next to him, the nuns whining about their connecting flight to Palm Springs or some other nun paradise, and the PA telling him to hurry up, hurry up, get there faster, faster, faster.

The girl will die if he does not fly faster.

"It's his job to say that, you know," said Scott.

"But it's a shitty thing to do to a pilot," said Casey. "It's not like you aren't already freaked out enough."

"Your job to fly, his job to freak you out," said Scott.

"And save the girl," said Casey.

"It's everyone's job to do that," said Scott. "The PA just doesn't want you to forget it."

"Her mother screaming in my ear the whole time," said Tony. "How could I forget it? Even if I wanted to, how could anyone forget it?"

So the weather is absolute shit and he can't make a miracle happen, he can't part the clouds or make the sun shine through. Tony sucks it up anyway, just like he's supposed to, like he learned over and over again, and he keeps on flying. There are no instrument routes out there and no hole to punch up through the clouds anyway, even if there was one to aim for. He has to stay under it, avoid the taller hills, follow the river, and he's done this a million times anyway, right? He knows this place better than just about anyone. He *knows* this river. So he thinks it through: Follow the water and get to Tanana, then straight on over the flats to Fairbanks. Get the girl to Town and she'll live, and no one's ever gonna ask how you did it anyway. It's a medevac, no one's gonna ask. So do what you have to do, what any pilot would do.

Just get it done.

And when he looks back to see how it's going with the girl; when he turns his head to make sure she isn't already dead, he sees the nuns looking out their windows, staring off into the clouds and the rain without any sign of praying on their faces. No beads clicking in their laps, no clutching of crosses or Bibles. It was clear to Tony right then that they weren't working their nun hotline to God on behalf of Amber Durrell. They were just checking their watches and tapping their toes like anyone else who wished they were already there. Obviously they wanted Tony to fly faster too, but not for the girl; they didn't even notice she was back there anymore. Those two nuns on their way home weren't giving a moment's thought to the girl on the stretcher behind them.

They weren't thinking about her or him or anyone else but the flight they didn't plan on missing. They were thinking about a different kind of flying altogether, about the end of Alaska and the beginning of where they wanted to be.

The whole time the nuns ignored her, Amber's mother kept trying to reach God on her own in the copilot's seat. She kept trying to get someone in Heaven to hear her while the Church slipped away from seats staring at the back of her head. Seats so close they could touch her, but long gone and miles away from this emergency; long gone from anything that would help this particular mother in her sad little moment of need.

Fucking nuns, thought Tony as he turned away, useless fucking nuns.

He got back in record time and called the tower with the "Lifeguard" call sign, and they put him down with priority clearance, got everyone else the fuck out of the way; even Alaska Airlines had to wait. The ambulance was already at the Company, and Amber was gone just like that, off to Fairbanks Memorial, and Tony didn't know if she lived or died that night because his job was done now. He was all about the flight, and his job was done.

The nuns didn't thank him as they jumped into the van for a ride to the main terminal. They didn't thank anybody for anything. They just drove away like they expected to; they just left Alaska behind like they had been planning to all along.

———•———

So it sounds like this pilot saves the girl, everyone goes home happy, and it's just like you read in the old bush pilot books. Right now you're saying to yourself, *I knew that was what they did up there; I knew those pilots were heroes.* It would be even better if I could write that Tony was changed by the flight, that it deeply touched him, that he came in the door and he was high as a kite over it, thrilled by what he had accomplished. That it has rocked his world. But that would be a lie, because when it was all over and done with, Tony was already halfway to forgetting about Amber Durrell. Funny, but this would have been a better story if he had.

It would have been better if all of us had.

Okay, here's the epilogue:

Amber and her mother come out to the Company a week later to fly back home. And we were all happy to see the kid looking so good, walking around and laughing and talking to everyone. We couldn't believe it was the same girl. And Tony came up and he saw them there and talked to the mother, and wasn't it just beautiful how they were all together again, just beautiful. And when he came back we all wanted to know what the mother said. We were thinking she must have been thanking him, must have been telling him how grateful she was for all the regs he busted and chances he took to get her kid into Town in time. But we were so wrong, so fucking wrong.

Turns out we were all a bunch of idiots when it came to Amber Durrell.

The kid did in on purpose. That's what Tony told us; she did it on purpose. "Stupid little bitch wanted tickets to the fair, so she grabbed every pill in her mother's medicine cabinet and swallowed them," said Tony. "She got herself good and overdosed so she'd get a free ride paid by the insurance because mommy wouldn't pony up the money for plane tickets. She wanted to go on the carnival rides with her friends, and her mom couldn't afford it. Getting a medevac meant the flight would cost them nothing."

Can you believe it?

We just stood there, all of us with our mouths hanging open. Tony was telling us this shit story, and we could not believe it. All those passengers gave up their seats, the schedule screwed up for the rest of the day. Tony flying around out there way too damn low for anyone's comfort, and it was all for a day at the Tanana Valley Fair. It was all for the Ferris wheel and cotton candy.

"And here's the kicker," said Tony, "the really funny part. The mother figured that since they were here anyway and Amber wanted to go to the fair so bad, they might as well have a good time, make the whole trip worthwhile. So she took her. They spent three days there as soon as the hospital cut her loose."

And that's it. That's what a real mercy flight is like up here. You have two nuns who won't give up their seats for a girl who ODs to go to the state fair for free and a mother who screams all the way that her baby is dying and then has a mini-vacation with her on the Tilt-a-Whirl as a reward for getting scared half to death. And now Tony's supposed to go back out there and fly them all home and act like it doesn't matter, like it doesn't just piss him off so bad that he can hardly stand it. And the Bosses say what the hell, we got paid for it right? We got our money. It's a good flight, because we got our money.

It was always a good flight when the Company made money.

—·—

So that's the story of Amber Durrell. I don't know if she's dead or alive now. It's been a few years and she wasn't making good choices back then, so who knows if she got smarter. I know when I ran into Tony and told him I was writing about this, there were a some things about it that he couldn't remember. The one thing he told me for sure though was to put in the part about the nuns. "I should have dropped them off in Ruby," he said. "I never should have brought them in to Town.

"Fucking nuns."

10

Dropping through a Hole in the Sky

There was a chief pilot at the Company a few years before I got there, a guy I knew only in passing. He was fired after cracking up an airplane on landing. He had a bad habit according to the stories, a scary stupid habit. In crap weather he would take off for a village that required you to file IFR to the nearest airway fix in order to legally get in the area. He would fly solid in the clouds, but when he got near his true destination, he would start looking for a hole, a way to get down to the ground. He would look for an opening in the clouds, and then he would cancel his flight plan because he no longer needed it and drop down. He would corkscrew the aircraft into as tight a turn as he could to make it through the hole, thinking he knew where he was but never certain, never sure.

He did this in the middle of mountain ranges, and he did it all the time.

Because he was lucky he thought he was good, and he kept flying airplanes in and out of clouds like he knew exactly what he was doing and where he was, even when there was no way that could be true. He was the Company Chief Pilot and in the air he was always the captain, and he thought that made him smarter and wiser than everyone else. He believed the title alone *made him good.* But no one else thought so, and one by one the guys that got stuck flying as his copilot had a moment of personal clarity where the question was clear: Was another man's luck enough to bet their life on?

Dale was an older pilot with the Company at the end of a flying career that went back forever. He had more than one war behind him, more than one moment of near dying in the sky over someplace most of us had never heard of. He didn't think he had anything left in him to scare, but then shortly after he was hired, he drew a turn as copilot with the old C.P.

"He pulled that crap on me one day going into Anaktuvuk," Dale told us later. "He started poking around, looking for somewhere to drop down. I told him it was solid and that was it; we either go all the way north until it breaks up and come back underneath, or we turn around and bag the whole thing. Those are the only two choices we have. And he says I don't know what I'm talking about. There's no better way up there," said Dale, shaking his head. "Never any better way in country like that."

"So what did you do?" Scott asked.

"He starts talking again about coming out of those clouds, and I told him that wasn't the way we were going to fly. Go north or turn back, one or the other, that's what I told him. He says I'm wrong, and I told that son of a bitch that he might have more ideas than God but I didn't have to listen to them, and I sure as hell didn't have to sit there and let him fly me into the side of a mountain. And then he says he's captain, like that's the end of it. Like I should give a shit," Dale said, sitting back in his chair and looking at us. "Never let anyone talk you into the ground," he said. "It won't matter when you're dead that you didn't feel right about it; it won't matter that you didn't want to go along with it. You'll be dead and just as much to blame. But mostly you'll just be dead."

As it turned out, arm wrestling his copilot for the controls in midair was something even the CP didn't want to do. He turned the plane around. After they landed back in Fairbanks, Dale made it clear he wouldn't give him a second chance. He told the CP he was going to kill somebody someday, and it sure as hell wasn't going to be him.

"Not me, not for someone else's stupidity," he said to the memory of it. "Never for someone else's kind of stupid."

But Dale was probably the only one who had the time and experience to be intimidating on words alone. Everybody else was stuck with having to prove their point using much clearer terms; for Tony that meant threatening to pull his gun.

"It's the middle of winter and we're going into Galbraith Lake and it sucks like always and I knew what he was going to try and do; I just knew it," he said. "He points out this tiny hole a few thousand feet below us, and I can barely see the thing. He can barely see the thing, but he says he's going to cancel the flight plan and drop down into it, and I said no fucking way, no way in hell are we doing this. And he starts giving me that captain shit, about how he has done this a thousand times before and he can judge what is safe and what's not, and I told him his idea of safe was a hell of a lot different from mine, and then he tells me to shut up."

"Sit there and look pretty," says Dale. It's an old joke, and everyone who has flown copilot more than once has heard it.

"Yeah," agreed Tony, "like I'm gonna do that. I figured I had two options: Let him fly through that hole and take my chances along with all the poor bastards sitting behind us who had no clue, or make him stop. Talking wasn't doing any good, so all I had left was to force him. I opened up my flight bag and told him to look inside, and right there is my pistol. He knows I fly with it, and he knows I know how to use it. And I told him, he wants to kill himself, well fine—he can fly himself into the ground any damn day he pleases. But not today, not with me sitting there. And if I need to, I'll pull that gun out and shoot his ass if that's what it's going to take."

They came back from Galbraith without landing, and Tony didn't get scheduled as the CP's copilot anymore either. "He always had to push it," said Tony. "Like he didn't think it was hard enough anyway, like he needed taking that extra chance to really make it all worthwhile."

The old chief pilot started scheduling himself with the new hires after that, the ones who didn't know enough to be scared. "But then he gets stupid," says Tony. "And he schedules himself with Alex, and that guy might have been new to Alaska, but he was crazy for a hell of a long time before he ever got here. They start going for a hole in the same dogshit as always and Alex doesn't say a single word, not a warning, nothing; he just reaches into his bag and pulls out his gun. He points it at the CP and tells him not to even think about it, and even after he turns the plane around, Alex keeps the gun on him. He doesn't say a word, not a single word for miles until they get on the ground in Fairbanks and he tells the CP he doesn't think he'll be flying copilot too much anymore, and that's the end of it. Alex goes right up the seniority line overnight."

"Crazy meets crazier," said Dale, shaking his head.

"But the owners still kept him as CP," said Tony, "because they liked it when he got in—they figured any risk was worth letting that son of a bitch fly."

"It's easy for them to decide from back here, in the office, though, isn't it?" I said. One thing I'd noticed real quick was that everything was easier from the ramp, especially the flying.

I used to wonder if that old CP would have been the same kind of pilot anywhere else. Was he just crazy and that's why he liked flying in Alaska, or was it flying in Alaska that made him that way? If he wasn't in a place that let him get away with those kinds of risks, would he have had to fly safe in order to keep his job?

Of course none of that mattered after he screwed up that landing. That maneuver cost the Company a lot of money and worse, brought up all kinds of questions from the Feds about judgment and safety.

Nobody likes it when the Feds start officially declaring your chief pilot stupid.

So the Owners were sorry but he had to go, and that was the end of it. By the time I was hired he was already flying for somebody else out of Nome, and no one thought about him much except to tell the stories. We did wonder though if he was doing the same shit out there; if they were letting him do it, wanting him to do it.

And then we knew for sure how it was.

The old CP was flying the line in Nome as a single pilot in a twin-engine for the new company, no more copilots to tell him what not to do. It was crap weather one day in December, and he decided to go take a look with a load of passengers to see if he could get in anywhere. It was legal to fly out of Nome VFR—the ceiling was thirty-five hundred feet with seven miles visibility—but to get into Koyuk he had to fly over some mountains, if he chose to go direct. Even in bad weather it shouldn't have been hard to reach Koyuk the long way; getting there along the coast should have been the easy part. But there were signs that maybe corners were being cut at this company, that taking chances wasn't something a few pilots did on occasion but what everyone did all the time and it was no secret. The Nome station manager told the Feds that all the guys flew with handheld GPS devices; it was common practice, something they used to help them get in.

They punched in the coordinates, and when they couldn't see they let the GPS tell them where to go. They flew it like most people drive; they flew it like it knew everything.

They flew it, and they got used to flying in anything.

The old CP had his own GPS, but he left it in another plane that day and ended up borrowing one from another pilot. It took him on a straight shot from Nome to Koyuk, right over the mountains. And even though he knew the area—everyone who flew into Nome knew those mountains were there—he and that GPS flew right up to Mount Arathlatuluk at 2,995 feet. And then he flew into it, straight on, full speed, 170 knots, impacting the side at the 2,725 level. He was less than one mile from the peak, in a place where everybody knows the mountains, where everybody knows that you have to fly thousands of feet higher than he was flying. Draw a line on a map east out of Nome and you can see where he crashed; you see it and you wonder how in the world a pilot could forget those mountains were there.

Even if you can't see where you are going, still you always have to know *where you are*.

The state troopers traveled to the crash site on snow machines and reported later that it was "ceiling undefinable, visibility very poor, heavy snowfall, blowing snow." From the initial impact point, they could not see the main wreckage, which was all of 205 feet away.

If you can't see the mountains well enough to fly through them, then you climb as high as you have to in order to clear the peaks. That is what you do if you're out there in it and you can't see; legal or not, you climb as high as you have to in order to stay alive. That is what any reasonable person would do anyway, any good pilot. It's what anyone who still knew how to fly careful would be damn sure to do.

If there was anybody who would fly blind into a mountain range, though, it was the old CP. If there was anybody who believed the mountains would move, that the obstacles would disappear, it was he.

"He used to drop down through those holes in the middle of the Brooks Range," said Scott, shaking his head, "and you couldn't be sure in the middle of it what was down there. You couldn't be sure at that place, at that moment, that it was the right thing to do."

"It wasn't," said Tony. "It wasn't ever the right thing to do."

The official cause for the crash was classic in all that it didn't say: "VFR flight by the pilot into instrument meteorological conditions (IMC), and his failure to maintain sufficient altitude or clearance from mountainous terrain." What we all knew it should have said was "Pilot had a god complex that prevented him from making good choices; he thought the earth would move for him. He was wrong."

"Nobody knows what's out there," Dale said, "on a night when the snow is flying and the ground is gone. Nobody knows."

And they shouldn't act like they do either.

11

With Saint-Ex in South America

Until the Company, I never thought about the business side of the U.S. mail. But for the airlines on the East Ramp, the mail was the most important thing they moved; it was everything. Cold, snow, wind, or ice fog, the mail had to move. It came in priority sacks and boxes and the oddest assortment of packages of all shapes and sizes. A bike with a tag hanging from the handlebars, a tire with a tag taped to the side, a box of live baby chickens, an empty dog crate, cases of pop and duffle bags of clothes; all of them were U.S. mail. Not moving the mail on its scheduled flight meant risking having to transfer it to another airline, and unless the weather was unflyable for *everybody,* no one cared what our reasons for sitting on it might be. Screw up on delivery for a destination often enough and it would get pulled permanently, and without those government checks, most of the routes were money losers.

The passenger lists were a secondary concern every morning; what we waited for, what we had to know, was the mail. You could have a sixty-three-pound tripack stack of banded pop that fit nice and tight in a compact space or sixty pounds of boxed potato chips that overflowed out of the cabin. The numbers fooled you, and not until you saw what the boxes looked like did anyone know what was really going on with a flight.

So every morning before six o'clock the three of us—cargo, ops, and pilot—would huddle in the front office and decide what the load should be for our main scheduled flight: the all-cargo run downriver. Most days we could pack it floor to ceiling, and we needed it to be as tight as possible to reduce the pressure on the next downriver flight, which was our main passenger flight. Anything left behind would have to go down another way—or be hidden from the post office so that we didn't lose it to the competition.

Incidentally, we were all very good at hiding mail.

The mail kept the airlines flying in Alaska; it has always been the only real guaranteed moneymaker. Without those reliable government dollars, it would be too expensive for passengers to fly anywhere and the villages would be cut off most of the year. It's a crazy way to do business, but when I was working at the Company just one 51.85-pound box for Nulato would cost the person who mailed it $6.57 to send nonpriority, but the post office paid us $89.18 to move it. That was why the Company, along with every other airline in the state, worshipped the post office like God. And the postal service demanded that kind of devotion from the very beginning. It demanded Alaska aviation do whatever it took to make the post office happy.

That wasn't Ben Eielson's fault though. I blame Ralph Wien for the twisted relationship with the post office that all of us ended up trapped in.

—•—

On May 23, 1928, Ralph Wien had a total of ten hours of flight time, dual and solo combined. (The FAA currently requires thirty-five hours minimum for a private pilot license; Ralph would have needed more than that to fly commercially.) His older brother Noel was one of Alaska's aviation trailblazers, and they had started a flying service together and won a territorial contract to conduct three special mail flights between Fairbanks and Nome in the spring of 1928. Noel was missing that May on the Barrow charter with Russ Merrill, and although there was a dedicated search going on for him, the post office still had a strict timetable for the contract. Regardless of the reason, if Wien Alaska Airways could not complete the delivery of the last load of mail to Nome and other points on the Seward Peninsula, then all hope of future air mail contracts for their airline would be in serious jeopardy. No matter what kind of trouble Noel was in, Wien Alaska still had to move that mail, and Ralph was the only one there to do it.

The airline had just one available aircraft for him, an open cockpit biplane with no operating brakes or instruments. Ralph had only been to Nome twice, in 1925 and 1927, and both times as a passenger. On top of everything else he was quite ill that May with a cold that his family characterized later as "bordering on pneumonia." But still, to keep the Wien Alaska air mail contract, he climbed into the OX-5 Waco 9 aircraft and he flew.

Almost thirty years later, his sister-in-law Ada recounted the flight, writing that when Ralph landed in Nome, "he was so exhausted from strain because of his lack of experience, exposure in the open plane and heavy chest cold, he could not talk or get out of the plane for many minutes." After medical assistance that night, he flew again the next morning and delivered the mail to villages on the peninsula. He encountered heavy fog more than once, and that left him often unsure of his location (without instruments he literally was flying completely blind), but he made it back to Fairbanks by May 29 and the contract was fulfilled.

"We believe this to be one of the most courageous and difficult flights in the cause of Alaska aviation," Ada wrote in the Wien Alaska Airlines company magazine in 1956. "Successful completion of these flights helped greatly to prove the feasibility of air mail service for Alaska."

What it also proved was that Alaskan pilots would do anything—*anything*—to preserve a mail contract. Willingness to fly sick in a broken airplane through bad weather conditions with little training and experience was not only part of the job, it was a requirement. The mail was more important than the rules and safety, and at the Company that was still true; it was true for everyone.

Ralph Wien's wife fainted when he left Fairbanks on the Nome flight; she was probably terrified that he would not return. As it turns out, Ralph died two years later while taking off from Kotzebue in an experimental airplane. But Wien Airways flew on for decades, and it kept receiving mail contracts.

———•———

When Antoine de Saint-Exupéry wrote about flying the mail in South America, he used his own experiences flying in the region for the French carrier Aéropostale as his guide. His resulting novella, *Night Flight,* is as much about the station chief, Rivière, as it is about the pilots. Rivière's determination to maintain the integrity of the schedule through any and all tragedy is what makes the routes successful, but it forces him to carry a particular burden and become a particular sort of man. He embraces duty and teaches everyone else that duty is paramount not only to the job's success but their own personal happiness as well. He teaches everyone this essential truth through example, and they believe in it, even as they wait in vain for the doomed pilot Fabien, caught in a cyclone; still they believe enough in duty to prepare for the next departure.

Always, Rivière knows, there is another departure.

Saint-Ex first flew for Aéropostale in 1926, and seventy years later I sat at a battered metal desk that could have been Rivière's and looked sideways at the chalkboard on the wall behind me trying to figure out who was behind, what planes were broken, and how long the crap weather we were dealing with was going to screw up the schedule. The board had the flights listed for the day, the clipboard held the mail still on the floor, the two rows of slots under the front counter had the freight slips, and the binders stacked along the wall kept the lists of passenger reservations. All of it waited for the next flight, for the perfect plan that never seemed to arrive. We might as well have been in Buenos Aires or launching Ralph Wien to Nome for all that the late twentieth century affected our lives.

My sense of duty to the people I worked with at the Company, with its sagging chairs, scratched desks, timed-out airplanes, and pissed off agents, had me impatient every day for what came next. Rivière was driven to deny the weather itself, daring pilots to challenge their assignments despite the conditions. "It was no concern to Rivière," Saint-Ex wrote, "whether he seemed just or unjust. Perhaps the words were meaningless to him. The little townsfolk of the little towns promenade each evening round a bandstand and Rivière thought: *It's nonsense to talk of being just or unjust toward them; they don't exist.*"

He had his schedule to think about while I sat and stared at my board. We were alike that way, in our subservience to routes we never set, times we did not choose, and weather we perpetually hated because it was not ours to control. Pilots I could argue with, Maintenance I could beg, Owners I could defy, but the weather? The weather didn't work for anybody. Rivière knew that, but in 1929 in the South American world of French aviation, he could ignore the weather. Even in Alaska, where everyone is convinced the rules are different, I didn't have that kind of power.

My board mocked me while I sat at my desk; constantly revealing all the ways my schedule must be met and how I would always fail.

When I read about Rivière, I wondered if Ralph Wien had ever considered the craziness of his flight to Nome. It was not the sheer audacity of the attempt that stunned me but how he defied the near absolute certainty that he was likely to die along the way. Rivière would have told him not to consider such deep thoughts; he would in fact have banished them from any conversation. "I am saving him from fear," Rivière thought about one of his pilots. "I was not attacking him but, across him, that stubborn inertia which paralyzes men who face the unknown. If I listen and sympathize, if I take his adventure seriously, he will fancy he is returning from a land of mystery, and mystery alone is at the root of fear. We must do away with mystery."

Ralph Wien must have convinced himself he was flying not to a place he barely knew, not along a route that was less real to him then a line on a map, but to the familiar, the routine. He couldn't be afraid just as Saint-Ex must have defied his own very real fears. You must lose all mystery while flying in places like Alaska or the Andes; it must be lost to duty. Rivière's message was clear: If you lose the mystery, only then may the flight succeed.

———•———

After that early downriver flight was gone, the cargo guy and I started on the others, sorting out the perfect mix of passengers, mail, baggage, and freight. I checked in the passengers, talking to them about their visits to Town, their kids, and always, the weather. The morning pilots hovered, alternating between going outside and getting their planes preflighted and watching to see who showed up and what might be loaded. They knew the plan for every flight was constantly changing, shifting with the needs of the load, the pilot, and the weather. I knew what the schedule demanded, but most days we changed the route. There was no reason to stop at a village if we had no passengers or mail for it. The variables spun in my head as everyone filled the area around Ops talking about the winter carnival or the state fair or what was on sale at Fred Meyers. The pilot waited until I closed the flight out, until the cargo guys told me what really could fit, until the list was set of everything and everyone that was going.

The flight did not belong to anyone else until I determined how to put all that information together, wrote out the load manifest, and made the numbers add up to a total that worked with what the pilot told me he could take. That's when it belonged completely to him and I became again just the one back in Ops who sent them on their way.

For me, it could only be paper; that's what the Bosses said from the beginning. If the pilot took that flight, with all the questionable numbers buried within it, that was his choice. "You just write what you have to so we can get that plane in the air." they told me. So that was what I did from the first day on the job; before I had any idea what I was doing, I wrote down whatever I had to. And if some of the pilots were leery of the numbers, suspicious of the difference between what I wrote and what they saw on their plane, then they had a decision to make. They could take it or leave it.

It was never supposed to be this way, not in the aviation world that I learned about in school. It was never supposed to be a question of what I would do to the guys I worked with.

No one will trust you, said the Owners. They don't want to trust you, said the Bosses. Operations always lied; it was part of the job. But I stood there in the morning, adding up numbers with cargo and the pilot standing beside me, and every morning we made a choice. I wrote a number down on a scrap sheet of paper and let the pilot see it—a number that matched nothing else, a number only the three of us knew. And then the pilot had that number and he made his choice, and that was how we flew.

Ralph Wien would call all these flights an act of courage, and Saint-Ex's Rivière would say they came from a sense of duty that could not be denied. The chalkboard and I didn't care. We just wanted the damn flight gone so we could get on to the next one. Thinking about the mail once it left wasn't what I was paid to do, and dwelling on boxes of freight was something that none of us had time for. But more than anything, I didn't want to be called a liar. We all had to make our own way at the Company, and writing down the number for the pilot was how I made mine.

Rivière would consider me a fool, and I'm okay with that. But Saint-Ex would have understood; good man that he was, I like to think he would have appreciated the moments of honesty in a job that had little to spare.

12

The Good Pilot

My friend Adam was a good pilot flying for one of the larger cargo companies in the state, and then one day, on a routine run into Bethel, he crashed. "The weather had turned to shit," he said afterwards, but it wasn't really bad—it wasn't the worst he'd ever seen. "I was bringing it down, shoot- ing the approach just like I knew it, and then that was it, I wasn't flying anymore."

"You crashed," I said.

"I was crashing," he corrected. And it wasn't until the plane stopped moving that he believed he wasn't going to die. He and his copilot sat there, stunned, both of them breathing like there wasn't enough air left in the world. It was quiet, he remembered later, but the shock in his head filled up everything; it was enough sound to fill the world.

That moment when Adam realized he survived was the last good thing to happen in his life.

At first the accident didn't make any sense. Adam didn't get behind the airplane, he knew the area, and he didn't ignore the weather. But good pilots don't usually crash for obvious reasons like those; it's more subtle for them. It's about more than the way things look from the ending. Adam knew his accident really started long before Bethel, but he didn't tell the Feds that when they asked their questions. His was the kind of truth that required patience; it was complicated truth, and the Feds don't do complicated. "Pilot error" was what they saw right from the beginning, and Adam knew that was how it would be. He argued a little, just because he knew he should, but he figured out quick the best thing to do was just to sit back and take it. He kept his secrets personal because they were his and they had nothing to do with Bethel. The Feds didn't need to know everything that made that crash happen.

When it was all over he lost his tickets, his job, his career, and his family. He lost everything, and it was only then that Adam's crash finally stopped, when everyone and everything was gone and the silence truly was complete. He could hear his heartbeat then; just his own heart and nothing else.

It made not dying in the crash seem like the worst joke in the world.

———•———

When I sat down to write this, I called Adam and told him I wanted to know the rest. I wanted the whole accident from start to finish.

"I had a fight with Teresa the night before," he says, and I can hear him shaking his head.

"So tell me," I reply. "Tell me how a fight with your wife brought you down."

"It's not that easy," he says. "The fight was just one thing; the last thing."

He starts talking about months before the accident because that is how he has to tell it. He starts the story back when his company upgraded to the new plane, when he became one of only two full-time captains in it, when he decided to try and time out by Thanksgiving. He wanted fourteen hundred flight hours by the end of November, and the Company was happy to give it to him. Six days of flying every week, if he'd take it. It was the Bosses' problem how to cover the schedule once Adam was timed out; he just wanted to fly himself into a month-long vacation; he wanted what every Alaskan pilot aims for.

"I was tired," he says, "from the fight the night before and the flying that week and the whole damn day. It was a long-ass day." And then he stops for a minute and remembers how it was. "I was tired all the time back then," he says.

Adam was on his third round-trip flight between Anchorage and Bethel that night, and his second copilot. Each leg was an hour and a half of flight time, but it hadn't been hard flying; the weather was holding up. But still it had been a long day, and it came after a long night before. He didn't even know how tired he was; he didn't know how close to trouble he was.

"Were you thinking about the fight a lot?" I ask.

"Not then," he said. "Not when I was on final trying to deal with that crosswind and looking for the runway lights. Nobody's thinking about anything then."

"But before," I say to him. "What were you thinking about before you hit final and it all started going wrong?"

"I just remember wanting to salvage the flight; wanting to get in." He stops for a minute because he knows what that sounds like; he knows how old this story is he's telling. Once you think about saving the flight, you're flying for the Bosses and not yourself; you're thinking more about the ground than the sky.

"I was thinking I only needed to get this one over with and a few more weeks of flying and then I'd be done for the rest of the year and then everything would be okay. Whatever was wrong I could fix then; I'd have time to fix everything then."

"So you did have the fight on your mind."

"Yeah," he says. "Back when I was still married and still had a house and a family, we had a fight. That was the night before the crash, and I was thinking about it.

"But not much," he adds. "Not enough to matter."

It was his fault and only his fault, and that was how he always saw it. You can't blame a crash like his on a fight—you can't blame it on anything but the pilot. But the fight did matter, and so did his schedule. When it came to understanding how Adam ended up skidding across the tundra, all of it mattered.

After the fight he only slept four hours—first because he couldn't stop thinking about how fighting seemed to be the only thing the two of them were good at any more and second because he was mad at himself for still fighting. They had wasted time on an old argument; one he was sure started months before but probably belonged to some distant point in their marriage that he couldn't even see anymore. He knew the fighting was pointless and there was no winning or losing, just the ritual of breaking apart, regrouping, and going at it again the next time. He knew all of this but couldn't seem to let it go, and so he didn't sleep well and that was the first thing about the crash, being tired.

Tired pilots make mistakes; Adam knew that, but it didn't make him fall asleep any faster. Tired also doesn't get anybody the day off, even when you know it should. The shit still has to move and somebody has to fly it.

"It was just a stupid pointless fight," he said. "It wasn't about anything; it wasn't going to change anything; it wasn't something I needed to think about. There was no reason to believe that fight was important."

"But you're still thinking about it now," I reminded him.

"Only because of the crash," he said. "If I hadn't crashed then the fight wouldn't matter, just like all the other ones before it never mattered."

He has forgotten the part where the fights brought him to the divorce. The crash was just one more stop in the road that ended his marriage, but Adam doesn't want to talk about that. The crash is an easier memory; it's one that makes more sense.

Anyone could understand that.

His first flight that day was in the afternoon; Ops told him to plan on three round-trips between Anchorage and Bethel.

"Everything at the office was just like always: Check the weather, the route, the plane, the load. Go outside, talk to my copilot, and maybe it was there in the back of my head, how pissed I still was at Teresa, but it wasn't important like the flight was. Once I got to work I was thinking about the job because the job was what was important. What Teresa did, what she might do, that was back at home. Once I got to work it was just the flying; there wasn't room for anything else."

But can you do that? Can you really leave it all at home, all the crap about who did what or said what or promised what and then forgot about it? Kids get sick and cars break down and garbage piles up, and you are supposed to just walk out the door and not see any of it? It's one thing to try and do that when your job is riding a desk, but it's a whole other deal when you're flying, especially when the weather goes down. It always has to be all about the airplane in the air, and Adam knew that; it was part of what made him good.

What used to make him good.

So that day the plane got fueled and loaded just like it always did, and they took off for Bethel and the weather was decent. They were VFR all the way, and Adam and the copilot took it easy, reading the newspaper, talking on the radio to the competition, bullshitting about the job. He and the copilot talked about December, when Adam was sure he'd be sleeping in every day. Plenty of time then to figure out his marriage, all the time in the world to do everything once he timed out.

"But what was it about?" I asked him now. "What was it always about with you two?"

"I don't know," he said. "But I'm sure she does; she always did."

Eight years later part of him would still like to blame the crash on her. He knows that wouldn't be honest, but still, part of him wishes he could.

The first trip was easy, and so was the second. But on the third trip, well into his seventh hour of flying, the weather started to go down. Just after 2100 hours they picked up the current recorded weather out of Bethel (which was eleven minutes old). ATIS Information "Charlie" reported "Wind 040 at 20, gust 28. Visibility 10. Ceiling 9,000 overcast." Bethel was still open for a VFR approach, but conditions en route were not.

An IFR approach into Bethel was nothing new, nothing to think hard about. Adam lived in Bethel at the beginning of his career; it was an airport that he literally could have flown into with his eyes closed. It would have been nice to have the last flight go as easy as the other two, but it didn't matter that much. "I'm just there to get it in," he said. "So I start thinking about the approach and keep flying. The sooner we were on the ground, the sooner we could start heading home."

"You were already thinking about getting out of Bethel."

"I was thinking about getting the flight done. That's the point; that's my job. That's what I was good at."

And he hasn't been as good at anything since, I know. That's the bitch of it when you're a good pilot. Once you stop flying, it's hard to be that good at anything else.

Seven minutes after they got "Charlie," Anchorage Center cleared them to three thousand feet and reported visibility in Bethel was "rapidly dropping." They should expect the localizer DME back course approach. They reported they had the airport in sight and were twenty-eight miles northeast of the Bethel VOR.

Five minutes later, twelve miles northeast of the VOR, Anchorage Center cleared them for the approach and to contact Bethel ATC.

Later, on the cockpit voice recorder, the Feds heard them talking about the approach, laughing about how screwed up it was out there, complaining about the weather. The copilot was excited; the Bethel back course was something new for him. Adam just sounded like Adam—like he knew what he was doing and was going to keep doing it, crosswind be damned.

Two minutes later the copilot checked the weather again, but the ATIS was silent. Later the accident report noted the weather was going down so rapidly Bethel was updating at that time with new information. But Information "Delta" would not be up until after the accident.

Three minutes later they were at three thousand feet as assigned by Anchorage Center and contacting Bethel ATC, which subsequently cleared them for the back course. They continued to the next step down of eighteen hundred feet for NAPAC Crossing, the initial approach fix. The copilot said he thought the approach was "pretty cool."

"The crosswind was a bitch," said Adam. "The autopilot was behind it the whole way down, trying to keep the course but always playing catch-up and never making it."

"Had you ever seen worse?" I asked.

"Lots of times," he laughed. "All the time."

Four minutes later they contacted Bethel tower and were told to report over NAPAC and the controller explained, ". . . uh, visibility has dropped down to about a mile, with, uh, light snow and the ceiling twelve hundred broken." The wind was over twenty knots.

"Could you see the airport then?" I asked.

"Couldn't see anything," he said.

"But it was still good."

"It was still Bethel," he said.

One minute later they were at eighteen hundred feet. Adam asked for the next assigned altitude. The copilot checked and reported "460 feet at NAPAC"; once past that point they could start down to the minimum descent altitude.

At 2128 they lowered the landing gear and put the flaps down to twenty-five degrees. They reported the NAPAC intersection. The tower responded they were not in sight but cleared them to land. Adam started a rapid descent of one thousand feet per minute. One minute later the copilot cautioned him that their airspeed was high. Between seven hundred and eight hundred feet, Adam disengaged the autopilot and began to hand-fly.

"The autopilot couldn't hold the course at all," he said. "We were getting bounced all over the place in those winds and the plane was chasing the course, always behind it."

"Could you see the ground now?"

"Still couldn't see anything."

"But you thought you would find it."

"If we got low enough," he said. "The ground always shows up."

He stopped and thought about that then—remembered it. "I just wanted to salvage the flight and get it down," he said, and any pilot could understand this; anyone could see what he was doing.

"But you could have missed the approach, gone around; set it up so you didn't have to come down so fast."

"I should have done that," he agreed. "But then I didn't think I needed to. I thought I could do it; I was sure I could do it."

"Were you thinking straight?" I asked.

"Apparently not," he said. "Apparently I wasn't thinking at all."

"So maybe you were too tired to know better."

"I was too tired to know anything," he corrected.

At 460 feet, Adam noticed they were left of the course. According to the data recorder, the plane leveled off at 21:29:36; six seconds later it started another descent that did not end until they crashed. The last altitude the copilot remembered was 390 feet on his altimeter. Sounds of impact were heard at 21:29:54. Neither one of them ever saw the airport or the ground. They were three and half miles from the end of the runway when they hit.

"I still don't know how it happened," he says. "I mean, I know I fucked up and it was my fault and I should have just gone around. But I didn't think we were that close. I don't know how we got there."

He thinks about that a lot; how you can be flying one minute and hitting the ground the next; how a crash can surprise you. How you can be so wrong without knowing it.

"You know the worst part though—the real bitch of it?" he says. "Now I'm one of those guys that I always used to laugh at, another asshole who couldn't keep his plane in the air."

But he's not; he's never going to be one of those guys. And that makes it even harder. Because he knows he was better, and he still crashed anyway. Even though he was the best on the line, he still destroyed a five-million-dollar airplane.

———

It played out just like Adam knew it would—the cause of the accident was pilot error due to "The captain's continued descent below the minimum descent altitude, which resulted in impact with terrain during an instrument landing approach." His tickets were suspended for twelve months, which might as well have been forever. His company offered to give him a desk job, but he didn't think that was right. "I didn't deserve a job there," he said. "What was I going to do—tell other pilots when they should fly? Who was going to listen to me?"

He said he quit to make it easier for everyone, but part of it was that he couldn't stand them all seeing him like that, like he wasn't any good. He didn't want anyone to look at him like that. It was hard enough to have to look at himself.

His new reality was that he was an unemployed pilot with no chance to fly for at least a year. He found out soon enough that when you're suddenly unemployed after some-how not dying in a plane crash, you spend a lot of time on the couch watching TV. You eat a lot of crap food and wear sweats and keep a cold beer within easy reach. This is when the people who care about you have to be patient because you could be on that couch for a long time; you could be stuck there for months. This is also when all those little fam-ily cracks and fissures start to widen or, in Adam's case, when your marriage, which was hanging by a thread, finally snaps. And then you're the guy who crashed and lost his wife and his house and, for way too much of the time, his kid as well.

The crash makes everything else so easy to destroy; it makes everything fragile.

"Nobody was flying that airplane," Adam told me. "I listened to the two of us on the CVR, and we were shooting the shit like we were up at fifteen thousand feet and didn't have a care in the world and there was nothing to do. I don't get it—I was there; it's my voice, and I still don't get it. If somebody told me they did this, I wouldn't understand how it could happen. It doesn't make it any easier trying to figure it out just because it happened to me."

That's the question dead pilots never have to answer: How did this happen to me?

His company survived, his copilot got another flying job, and Adam moved from a couch at home to a recliner someplace that wasn't home. He started throwing bags for Alaska Airlines and rented a storage unit for his half of the furniture that didn't fit in his new apartment. He tried to pretend he was moving on, but mostly he was looking back. He wanted his house again; he wanted his daughter doing homework in front of him every night; he even wanted those stupid fights. He wanted it all back, even though it hadn't been good, because whatever it had been, at least it was his.

"I keep thinking if maybe I could remember what it was we were always fighting about—what the big thing was that kept us going at it for so long—then maybe I would have been able to stop it somehow."

"Stop your marriage from breaking up?" I ask.

"Stop the crash, save the marriage," he says.

"You were there," I remind him; "it was your life. How could you not know what you were fighting about?"

"It's just a blur," he says. "There was something I was missing that I should have been doing. Something I didn't see."

Distracted in the air and you crash; distracted on the ground and everyone leaves.

"It was good once," he says. "We were happy."

And that was true too, but it didn't matter anymore. Everything about how it used to be didn't mean anything anymore.

"I was the best pilot at that company," he tells me, and I believe him. And when he says he is still one of the best, I believe that too. Everybody has a fight sometimes; everybody gets tired; everybody tries too long to be a company man. But what you can get away with on the ground and in the air are two different things—they're worlds apart, and that's the biggest part of what makes flying so hard. There's no room for all those little human failings up there, not when the weather can go to shit so quickly, not when you and the copilot aren't talking enough about flying, not when neither one of you can see the ground. There's only room for doing the right thing on final approach in a snow shower with a gusting crosswind; there's only room for knowing that you have to do the right thing.

"I don't know how it happened," he says. "How could I do that? How could I crash?"

"Would it matter?" I ask. "If you could explain it, would it matter?"

"It would be something," he says, looking around at what he has left. He works in a cubicle now in a place where no one understands what it means to be captain; what it means to be pilot-in-command. "At least if I knew, when I thought about it there would be something to make it clear.

"If I knew what to remember, there would be something I could try to forget."

And I wish I could help him. I really do because he was good once, and living with that is going to be the end of him one day. Knowing how much he lost is one day going to put him in the ground forever.

13

The Worst Cargo in the World

The first time I saw a sled dog shipped as freight, it was crammed with two others into a crate designed to carry a single dog. They came in from a village, and as the Company charged by the size of the kennel and not by the weight or number of dogs, the goal was always to try to fit as many of them as possible into the smallest crate. All you could see in that box were paws and teeth as the three of them whined and cried while waiting in the hangar. When they got picked up, the crate was tossed into the back of a truck and driven away. I have no idea how long it was before any of them were let out of that box.

At the Company, the freight was basically all those things that had to be shipped right away (envelopes of money, buckets of chicken, flats of live plants, or bags of prescription medicine) or couldn't be sent any other way (snow machines, boat motors, animal carcasses). We basically hauled anything anyone wanted to pay us to move, and while the hazmat regs always applied, what mattered most was if it would fit in the airplane. The rules were the rules, but practicalities took center stage: the tape measure, weight, and balance calculations and the uncompromising shape of every aircraft door. If we could make it work, then we would; and more often than not, that was what we did. Dead animals in garbage bags were gross but not impossible. It was the live ones I dreaded having to deal with.

Sled dogs are everywhere in Alaska, as common in the cities as they are in the villages and the mainstay of every animal shelter, rescue group, or pound. They averaged forty pounds on our flights and have longish coats; they live outside chained to doghouses, and the only time they run is when they are pulling a sled. Some people keep them as pets (even as house pets) and there is no reason they shouldn't be. If you raise them well, they are like any other dog. But because of their working history, because of the romantic myth that has grown around them, because it has just always been that way, you will find sled dogs in yards on the end of five-foot chains by the dozens and even the hundreds in Alaska. You will also find them casually dead, shot in the head and thrown in the trash when they get too old, too slow, or too expensive to feed.

This is not a pet, my dog-owning friends would tell me; it's a sled dog.

When I first went to work at the Company, we primarily flew sled dogs as freight for people who were buying or selling them. They were a commodity that was cheaply shipped by fitting as many into a single crate as possible. People dropped them off in those crates with no food or water hours before they had to fly. People on the receiving end didn't show up to meet the airplane when it arrived in Fairbanks, and on one occasion we had a crate with three dogs in it left overnight in our hangar. The night maintenance crew finally let them out and tied them up because they couldn't stand the yelping anymore. The guy who got them the next day threw the crate in the back of his truck without a second look back.

That was when we all started seriously talking about never flying sled dogs again.

When Ernest Shackleton went to Antarctica in 1914, he took ninety-nine "sledge dogs" with him. In her book *The Lost Men*, Kelly Tyler-Lewis described them as each weighing from sixty to more than one hundred pounds. They were "powerful animals who lunged, snarling, at all comers." Navigator Joseph Stenhouse wrote, "Thrashing seems a cruel method to employ as a reproof, but as kindness has had no effect, it is the only one." Shackleton's dogs were a mixed lot sent by the Hudson's Bay Company from Canada. To accomplish his goal of being the first to cross Antarctica from coast to coast, Shackleton decided to use 75 percent of the animals for food for the rest of his teams, something Robert Peary is the first to have openly acknowledged when planning his attempts to reach the North Pole.

Some of Shackleton's dogs were given to the Ross Sea party, who served as the support crew for the doomed mission. Ten of those men were abandoned on shore when their ship became trapped in the ice and disappeared in a gale. The men and their dogs continued their goal to stage food caches for the journey, even though Shackleton's attempt to cross the continent failed before it began and devolved instead into an epic tale of survival at sea. When the explorer returned to rescue the seven surviving Ross Sea party members in 1917, the survivors included several of those dogs, all of whom returned to Australia with them.

A photo in Tyler-Lewis's book shows three of the dogs on the voyage home. Not one of them looks to be less than eighty pounds; this is how big a sled dog had to be back then to get the job done.

When it came to the successful use of dogs in polar conditions, the people who lived there were always head and shoulders above the European explorers. Englishman Edward Maurice took a job with the Hudson's Bay Company in the Canadian Arctic in 1930 and quickly discovered how critical dogs were to a village's survival. He meticulously recorded use of the dogs, "born and bred as hunters and workers," in his memoir *The Last Gentleman Adventurer* and noted that a hunter's team varied in numbers according to his ability to feed them. A hunter only had as many dogs as he could provide for, and their care was paramount:

> *The husky dogs were hard workers and, provided they were kept in good condition, would hold a steady pace all day. Just as it was possible to grade Eskimo housewives by the state of the oil lamps, so a hunter might be judged by his team.*

When the people who lived in the Arctic regions still survived on subsistence, the health of the dogs directly correlated to the health of their owners and the larger community. Explorers who cared for their dogs in a similar manner found greater success. Roald Amundsen was the first man to reach the South Pole and the first to reach both the South and North Poles (he also was the first to traverse the Northwest Passage). He set out for the South Pole in 1911 with a team of five men and sixteen dogs; eleven of those dogs returned with him. The significance of choosing the right dogs and caring for them was not lost on Amundsen, who wrote: "The dogs are the most important thing for us. The whole outcome of the expedition depends on them."

All of this took place a long time ago, when Alaska was a place to survive in and the term "sled dog" meant Alaskan Malamutes, Greenland Dogs, and Siberian Huskies. (Amundsen took Greenland Dogs with him to Antarctica.) All these dogs were bred for pulling weight and traveling at a moderate pace. They were not speedsters and never would be; strength was what mattered. When people Outside think of sled dogs, it is these dogs they picture; but they are not the dogs I saw and not the ones that showed up forced into crates for the Company to carry.

———•———

Flying dogs as freight was bad enough, but sled dog charters were the worst. When the mushers pulled up in their trucks and started pulling the dogs out of their little cubbies in the back and chaining them up to load, the dogs would all start howling and jumping. Then they were hauled one by one up the steps and into the plane, where they were chained to the tie-down rings along the floor. The whole time this was going on, the dogs tried to get loose and at each other; and because they were filthy, they got everyone around them covered in their dirt and their smell. And then they started peeing and crapping all over the plane and one another.

It made the inside of the average aircraft about the most unpleasant place on the planet.

Without fail, at some point in the middle of every sled dog charter, two or more of the dogs would start trying to kill each other or, even worse, mate. That's when the pilot would tell the musher to get back there and break it up and the musher would always, without fail, refuse. By the time the dogs were unloaded, the smell was from some inner circle of hell, and the plane was useless for passengers for at least a day. The tarps were a mess, the pilot was pissed off, and the mushers never thought to be grateful. The dogs didn't know what to think; they were just tied up someplace new and waiting for a chance to run.

We flew all sorts of cargo at the Company: pallets of pumpkins, stacks of Pizza Hut pizza, and on one nerve wracking occasion, an entire multitiered wedding cake. We flew dead moose, dead bear, dead fish, and hundreds of five-gallon buckets of salmon roe that was destined for Asia. We shipped tents and kayaks for campers, rifles and cook stoves for hunters, and sourdough starter and espresso machines for rich men pretending to rough it in the wilderness. By the time I left the Company, there was only thing we refused to fly, without exception, and that was sled dogs.

14

The Map of My Dead Pilots

Anywhere, everywhere in Alaska there are reminders of dead pilots. You find them on street names and buildings: Merrill Field in Anchorage and Eielson Air Force Base outside Fairbanks. The airport in Kotzebue is named for Ralph Wien, who crashed there in 1930; the airport in Barrow is named for Wiley Post, who crashed there in 1935 with Will Rogers. There is a street in Fairbanks named for Harold Gillam, who crashed in 1943. Aviation accidents happen in the state with such regularity that they rarely make the front page of the newspapers. Don Sheldon, who crashed almost two dozen times but survived to die of cancer at the age of fifty-three, seems almost wrong somehow. He's not the kind of ghost an Alaskan pilot is supposed to become.

I was four thousand miles from Fairbanks when Bryce crashed. That June I was chasing the end of a phone call I received almost three years earlier, a call to come home. "Cancer" was the only thing I heard in the first call in 1996, and I kept hearing it again and again. All the phone calls that came after that one were echoes of the first. There was dying and surviving in every conversation and visit with my father. And then in April 1999 my brother called one last time and told me it was time to come home for a while, time to come until it was over. I packed up Eielson and Merrill and the rest, all the papers and books for the graduate thesis I thought I would write while I was gone. But Florida quickly became just about my father and brother and me as we felt our hearts disappear into a shadow all at once.

My father died on June 5, 1999. Six days later the phone rang, and Bryce, who had children of his own, was gone too.

———•———

By the end of June I was back in Fairbanks and way behind on my thesis. It's been so long now that I can be honest— I was set to graduate in December, the first draft was due in September, and I had not written a single word. All the books I brought to Florida, the copied pages from old newspapers and magazine, had never left my suitcase. But I was afraid that if I didn't write it that summer I might never write it; I might not care enough about it to even try anymore.

Instead of considering the careers of men from decades before, I lost myself in a more personal history. You think that being thirty means you can handle the loss of a parent, that you're maybe even prepared for it because you are out of the house and far from home. I was five years old again that summer though, treading water beside my father, clasping his shoulder out at the breaker line. He taught us to watch for waves in the distance, choose one we wanted, and get ahead of it before it rose up beside us. He taught us to be ready. Choose your wave early, he taught us. I was five years old and riding them in on his back with my brother beside us, and I listened and I learned.

He said you crack an egg carefully so you can catch any piece of the shell; do a crossword puzzle one square at a time, left to right; start your tomatoes inside in early spring; never be without a good book, never let a day go by without reading.

There was no replacing my father. I taped his library card to my wall; my brother put his last pouch of pipe tobacco in his truck. Separately we watched the Red Sox play that summer; neither one of us could imagine ever going back to his beach. I sat on the couch lost in my memories, and that was all I could bring myself to do. My professors told me I didn't have to turn in my thesis that September; desperately I knew more than anything that I did.

There have always been companies that collect dead pilots, airlines that rack up accidents with an awesome regularity. In late 1997 in Barrow a Cessna Caravan pilot told a brand-new employee to fuel only one tank on the plane.

The pilot, who was also the station manager, apparently never double-checked the fuel level in both tanks, nor did he deice the aircraft. The uneven weight distribution in the wings caused a stall on takeoff and took the pilot and all seven passengers into the Arctic Ocean, plus the coffin of the recently deceased family member they were escorting to the funeral. Seven months earlier, a pilot for the same company flew into the ground near the village of Wainwright with less than a quarter mile visibility. He had four passengers who had threatened to fly on someone else if he wouldn't take off. They all died with him. And five months before that, another one of their pilots flew into the ground near the village of Marshall while he was on a moose surveying flight with a state wildlife biologist. Neither one of them survived either.

That was an airline with a string of very bad luck.

I collected these accidents and others like them the summer my father died, spending nights with them piled around me in separate stacks for VFR into IMC, "continued flight into known adverse conditions," "failure to maintain adequate ground clearance," "failure to maintain adequate distance from mountainous terrain," "failure to maintain adequate distance from snow-covered tundra," and straightforward "mechanicals." I read the reports over and over, hunted brief mentions in newspapers; I looked for the common missteps, the repeated errors. We spent time together, those accidents and I. They were my solace and I their loyal companion, the only one interested in visiting all those paper graves.

Not one of the reports ever blamed the companies. Bad decisions always belonged to the pilots because those fateful last decisions, regardless of why they made them, were always theirs.

Before I could write my thesis, I had to interview one hundred working commercial pilots. What I wanted to know was simple: Had they ever been pressured by management, passengers, or the post office to fly? Did they see themselves as bush pilots as in the 1930s and 1940s? What did they think caused so many accidents?

Every pilot I talked to had something to say about the job—whether he thought it was easy or hard, if he loved or hated it, whether he was dying to get out or desperate to stay in. They thought the passengers were the problem, or the rules for moving the mail, or it was just the way things always had been and so it didn't matter if they wanted it to change because it never would. This was flying in Alaska, and some were happy about that while others were hanging by a thread.

A pilot in Kotzebue called me one night to say he was convinced his company was trying to kill him because they kept asking him to fly in crazy weather. Another from Bethel told me about a passenger who pulled a gun on him during a flight when the weather forced him to turn around. (The other passenger managed to persuade him that shooting the pilot was probably not a good idea.) They said that the post office threatened constantly to take the mail away; that the competition was crazy enough to fly in anything to keep the mail; that the planes were held together with glue and prayers; that the weather was never what they were told; and on and on and on. There were no easy answers, not from the pilots I never met, not from the ones I knew far too well, and not from the Feds who all that summer couldn't figure out why Bryce had crashed in the Yukon.

———

One night in July a group of us were out at the Chena Pump-house, holding court in the bar overlooking the water. Some of the guys were calling back and forth with the tourists on the riverboat as it approached the deck out back, and I was interviewing a pilot in town visiting friends. I explained my thesis, and she mentioned a company she used to work for in Kotzebue. I told her a friend of mine had worked for them there in 1995 until he crashed into a mountain. And then she put her beer down and said, "You knew him." Before I could stop her, she started talking about how crazy it was, how it made no sense, how the whole thing was such a huge waste.

And I kept thinking, you were there, you were there, you were there. And she said, sometimes these things just happen and you have to let them go. All I could think was, Why did this have to happen now? Why did Luke have to come back *this* summer?

"It was a stupid accident," she said, "a fucked-up mess."

"I talked to the Feds who went out there," I told her. "They said it was bad."

"He shouldn't have been there; took a wrong turn or something. It was just stupid."

"He didn't have a lot of mountain experience," I said, and then I forced it. "He didn't know better."

"Everybody knows better," she said, shaking her head. "That's why we couldn't figure it out. We all went looking for him, but he wasn't anywhere we thought he would be. How he got into that pass I'll never know. It didn't make any sense."

"He was chasing wolves," I said. "That's what the Feds wrote in the report."

"We were all chasing wolves," she said, looking at me. "Why would that matter?"

Nobody pressured Luke to fly that day, and nobody made him chase those wolves or fly low to see them better or not look up to see where he was or fly into that stupid mountain. But here was someone who was there, and she knew less than I did how he ended up in that canyon. She had talked to Luke that morning; she had seen him that morning and yet she still couldn't figure it out.

"We looked all over for him, but he wasn't where he was supposed to be. It was just really fucked up," she said. "Was he a good friend of yours?"

"An old friend," I said.

"Well, sorry about that; he seemed like a good guy." And then she drank some more beer and turned around to watch the boat.

Two of the drunker guys on the deck mooned the tourists and everyone started cheering. The voices in my head were louder than that though; they were louder than everything. Why did Luke's accident have to come back to me now?

The summer of 1999—just one wrong death after another.

———•———

The pilots I interviewed told me that flying was hard or scary or insane. They said it was easy and overrated and nothing exciting. They complained that their Bosses made them fly while the guys sitting next to them said they begged for as many hours as they could get. Each and every one of them was brutally honest and flagrantly lying, no exceptions. Interviewing those pilots was the most revealing, disappointing, and frustrating experiment I have ever been a part of. I never found out what makes them do the things they do; I only learned that there are always more willing to do it. There are pilots who will fly and nearly die because that is what the job makes them do, just as there are those who will never notice that the work is hard, let alone dangerous. They are all out there together, but they all see something different and they don't know why. No one does.

When I surveyed the data, it told me that an overwhelming percentage of commercial pilots in Alaska felt pressured for one reason or another to fly. They all knew it was their decision to accept that pressure, but the final result was a foregone conclusion. Modern rules were not what kept planes in the air in Alaska; decades of aviation history was. The one thing everyone agreed on is you can't make people forget all the times someone else got in, and you can't make them stop expecting the next guy to do it too.

It would have been easier to understand Luke's crash if someone else had been in that plane with him—someone who wanted to get home right away, someone who threatened him, someone who had made him fly into that mountain. A passenger would have explained why that kid I never met went into the side of Atigun Pass too. But their accidents were like so many others in Alaska, like Eielson's and Merrill's, even Bryce's. They were all pilots in the middle of nowhere who made their own bad choices and whether or not someone asked them to take those flights didn't really matter in the end.

"It was so stupid," that pilot I did not know said to me while we were sitting at the bar, like stupid made it easier to understand how any of those crashes happened.

—————

I've been writing about that summer forever, it seems, about the irony of meeting someone who brought Luke's accident back to me at the same time we were struggling with Bryce's. In the middle of it all was my father's death, so raw and recent that I couldn't leave it behind, even for a moment. I did not realize then that all I learned that summer would stay with me so strongly that twelve years later it would still be a summer I cannot forget. But typing that right now makes me see how foolish I was ever to think that time would change anything about it.

The truth is that whenever I write about my father's death, it's forever just five minutes, not nine or eleven or twenty years, that have passed in my life since he was gone.

And so the summer of 1999 and everyone I met and everything I learned is a frozen moment in time.

The whole litany of dead pilots is there with me too, all of us together in a summer that, no matter how hard I wish, will never fade away.

15
Getting Lost

Everyone thinks there are two different flying stories in Alaska: the way it was and the way it is now. Eielson and Merrill (and Wien and Gillam and Joe Crosson) are supposed to be ancient history. But where is the myth's breaking point, the moment when Bush flying should have grown up but didn't? Everyone knows aviation in the Lower 48 was wild back in the Lindbergh and Earhart days, but no one expects Delta or United to fly the same way now. There are rules, technically written, carefully enforced; pages and pages and pages of rules that everyone in aviation has to live by. And those rules apply just as equally to Alaska. But all I kept finding in the rolls of microfilm and binders of old magazines were more stories about heroes, more examples of the past forcing its way forward into every decade of the future. Lindbergh retired, Earhart disappeared, and still Alaskan pilots kept crashing in the same way, in the same places.

"Everybody needs a wilderness," said Frank. "Looks like you finally found where aviation keeps theirs."

"But there's nothing left to discover anymore," I argued. "The maps are written; the charts are set. We've got GPS for God's sake. You only get lost anymore if you want to."

"We've got all that, but we still don't know why Ray flew that plane out of gas or Bryce didn't put the plane down on a gravel bar," said Frank. "Lost isn't just a place, you know."

"Why the hell did I take so many flights when I knew I was too tired to fly," said Sam.

"And I left a warm office for the middle of nowhere when it was crazy butt cold out," added Scott.

"Here's your wilderness," said Tony. "It's in our heads and the Company rules and what the passengers want and post office demands."

"You know they always died in those Jack London stories," I said. "I don't need that kind of wilderness. Nobody does."

"If we're honest, it's the only kind there is," said Bob. "Fictional wilderness that we all end up in without even realizing it. The rest is just people pretending to be lost for their own stupid reasons."

"Yeah, and hoping we'll find them," said Scott.

"They're the ones who won't let it go," said Frank. "As long as they keep living the Alaska dream they picked, we've got to make it work."

"Even if that means hauling cases of pop to the Bush at fifty below?" I asked.

"Even so," said Frank, "even so."

And everyone nodded because they'd all done it and they'd all do it again if they had to, if it was their job to. Just like Eielson and Merrill and Wien, just like all the pilots that came before them.

———•———

When Ben Eielson made the first landing on the Arctic ice in 1927 with George Wilkins, he was 450 miles from anyone that could save them. His plane suffered engine trouble, and while Wilkins took depth soundings that proved to be a landmark moment in oceanography, Eielson struggled for two hours to repair the Stinson so that the two of them wouldn't freeze to death. He got it back in the air, but after turning back toward Barrow, the engine eventually quit again.

Based on a sun shot taken by Wilkins's sextant, they were more than sixty miles from help when they landed the second time. Over the next five days the two men hunkered down in a windstorm but did not receive any replies to their brief radio messages. With no rescue forthcoming, when the weather let up they decided to walk out. Thirteen days later they reached a trading post at Beechey Point, where they were met by a dog team. Two joints from Eielson's little finger would later be amputated due to frostbite, but the men survived. In 1928 they would fly north again and this time complete the first flight from America to Europe across the Pole.

That kind of wild—Eielson's wild—was the rule in his lifetime, and it continued to be long after he was gone. Harold Gillam flew in it his entire career. He had made only one distance flight in his life when he joined the search for Ben Eielson in 1929 and was alongside Joe Crosson when his airplane was found. He spent weeks out in the Siberian tundra helping in the long search and recovery of the bodies. Over the years he became infamous as the pilot with a near perfect record delivering the mail. The weather was never bad enough to keep Gillam on the ground. Eventually he got the nickname "Thrill 'em, Spill 'em, No Kill 'em Gillam." Passengers loved Gillam because he always got them home, even when everyone else canceled their flights. He stuck to the schedule above all else, and precious little was capable of grounding him.

In 1943 Gillam was flying a twin-engine Lockheed Electra for a construction company working contracts in Alaska. He took a flight out of Seattle with five passengers on January 5, heading to Anchorage. They ran into dense fog four hours later near Ketchikan and then lost the left engine. The plane hit severe turbulence, falling several thousand feet in a sudden downdraft. According to the passenger in the copilot seat, they broke out of the clouds at twenty-five hundred feet in time to see a mountain directly ahead. When the survivors were finally located four weeks later, Gillam and one of his passengers, Susan Batzer, were dead. The wreckage was not found sooner because, with the exception of a disjointed radio call right before impact, Gillam had not made one single radio report during his entire flight. No one knew where they were.

Gillam's body was not found with the wreckage; he died while attempting to walk out to the beach and find a rescue party. When one of his passengers later described the flight for the *Alaska Sportsmen,* he referred to the pilot as a "prince of men" and wrote that "no pilot anywhere has to his credit a more courageous and brilliant record than Harold Gillam." The *Polar Times* reported the accident under the headline: "Gillam, Hero of 100 Flights in the Arctic, Dies on Mercy Trip." In the same article, copied from the Associated Press, he is credited with discovering Ben Eielson's wreck by himself, "flying with the Aurora Borealis for light." The *Fairbanks Daily News-Miner* said Gillam gave his life for his passengers.

But this is only one version of the story, only one truth. The other is found in what the newspapers didn't report, in the forecast weather that grounded other flights heading north out of Boeing Field that day, in the fact that Gillam had only finally obtained an instrument rating the year before and was still notoriously deficient in standard approach procedures. He maintained radio silence during almost the entire flight, even after he was lost in the clouds, and he was pointedly unaware of the wartime practice of altering courses in and out of Annette Island, the new army field in the southeast that he attempted to reach as the weather deteriorated. This was a military policy he would have known if his charts were not obsolete. Most telling of all, in its investigation the Civil Aeronautics Authority determined the accident was due to pilot error, for Gillam's continued flight into the storm and his failure to use his radio.

Not one single Alaskan newspaper mentioned the CAA's report; in fact the *News-Miner* claimed he ran out of gas.

The last story about the Gillam crash is purely fiction. It's what passenger Susan Batzer would have told if she had lived, if the survivors had been found during the two days before she slowly bled to death while trapped in the wreckage. Her story would have started with "I have a new job in Alaska," and whether or not it would have ended with Gillam as a hero we cannot know.

All the contemporary news accounts spelled her name differently. I still don't know for sure if she was Susan Baxter, Balzer, or Batzer. In fact, other than knowing she died on Gillam's last flight, no one ever knew much about her at all. No record of her grieving family, no report of where she was buried or when. Meanwhile, Gillam's burial was front-page news.

At the Company we didn't talk about Gillam as much as understood that his commitment to always go take a look was what the Owners wanted—what all of the owners in fact depended on. Gillam proved in the 1930s that taking off was the surest way to guarantee completing a flight. Waiting around for better weather wouldn't get you anywhere and, more importantly, it wouldn't get the job done. That was what everyone remembered, even if they didn't remember him.

But that was all then—that was *them*. Flying into the wilderness was part of what those guys did, and if they were smart—when they were smart—they transformed the landscape from the unknown to the familiar. The only reason Harold Gillam died was because he didn't bother to know where he was. The truth about that crash is that Gillam was lost only because he chose to be. That's an important difference, for Gillam and Eielson and the old CP and Luke and the guy who flew into Atigun Pass I never met. It was not being where you thought you were or knowing how far away you were from what you knew that made the difference in a very bad way.

———•———

"Have any of you ever been lost?" I ask them.

They look at me and one another, and then Frank smiles and takes a drink.

"We're still here, aren't we?" says Scott. "Doesn't matter what happened out there if we're still here now."

There are two ways to tell a flying story: the truth and what everyone wants to hear. You can't have it both ways. The best stories try to walk a fine line, keep it real while making it funnier than it was, less frightening than you remember it. No one wants to hear how you saw Jesus. But telling a flying story is not the same as living one, not even close. The story is just the memory, the rose-colored glasses moment that you take out at parties and bars, that you use to lighten the atmosphere when the in-laws visit. The only requirement is that you can't be too serious; that's pretty much mandatory. No one wants it to be too real. Remember that; never let your story get too real.

That'll kill it for sure.

But I think if you tell a story enough, you can find the truth in it; you can find the way it really was and not just how you wanted it to be. The lies in a story don't come from wishing it was better. They come from knowing it wasn't. Ben Eielson made a mistake; so did Harold Gillam and Russ Merrill and hell, so did Bryce, and we just have to learn to live with that somehow no matter how hard it might get. Ultimately, the one thing that matters isn't what we hoped would happen, or want to say happened, or even what someone who wasn't there tries to claim happened. It's the truth we have to find, and in flying it's always there waiting for you in those last decisions and final moments, in the crash itself or what brought you to it.

We still tell stories about flying in Alaska, and we probably always will. Someday we'll finally get them right, most of them. But even if we don't, it will still be the truth we are hunting for and still the truth we hope to find. The flying was always the easy part for everyone; it's the remembering that will take us forever to forget.

16
What Happened to Bryce Donovan

There are only a few things we know for sure about the day Bryce died. We know his right engine struggled on the ground, that he turned back for the airport soon after takeoff, and that the last thing he said was he might have to ditch. That's enough to fuel a dozen different scenarios though, a dozen different possibilities of what really went on in the cockpit. We don't think about Bryce's crash much when we're on our own, but put us in a room together and we can't seem to help ourselves. There's no way we're going to fix it, no way that we can save him. But his crash is our war story now, and none of us know how to let it go.

Most days, we don't even seem to want to.

Because he was the first one there, Frank knew Bryce's story best. We listened to him because we were desperate and wanted anyone's story if it could tell us what happened. The problem was Frank didn't know any more than the rest of us. He knew about the right engine having trouble starting because that's what the agent said, and it made sense anyway. Of course there must have been an engine problem. What else would bring the plane down so fast? That's all we heard from the beginning: right engine, right engine, right engine. But then they didn't find the right engine in the river; it was gone along with the entire right wing, swept away by the Yukon. Without any other immediate answers, Frank's story then became the only story about Bryce's crash, and at first that was okay; it was enough. But eventually the rest of the airplane started talking, and we had to listen to that too.

It didn't help that there were complicating factors in the investigation. The fact that the airplane went into the river, into the Yukon River in particular, made every part of the recovery difficult. The divers never had more than four inches of visibility when they were in the water, and sometimes as little as two. The right wing could have floated right past them and they wouldn't have seen it. It probably broke off immediately after impact, taking the right engine away with it. We wondered sometimes if the wing ever washed up way downriver. There are broken airplanes all over Alaska; people use them as garden ornaments or interior design accents. It is not a place where an abandoned wing is noticed or reported. There was no reason to hope we would ever see that engine again.

So it always starts the same way, with everyone sitting around shooting the shit about nothing special. Somebody tells a story about something and everyone laughs until eventually the conversation comes around to the Company and someone mentions Bryce's name and tells a story that used to be his. And just like that, everyone is back there again, hearing the phone ring, walking through the Company like they're in a fog, and flying out to Tanana to see the wreck.

To wait until they find Bryce.

Just like that we are back there again, and then someone says he's been thinking about it and he thinks he knows what really happened. Then we all listen and take our turns. We all try to figure it out again.

None of us can help it. Even though we know it won't give us any answers, we still can't leave it alone. It's only a matter of time before we go back there again though, only a matter of time.

"This is how it happened," says Scott, and we try not to look too eager when he starts talking.

"Bryce took off from Tanana and he was angry, because the two passengers he was supposed to pick up had both overslept. The agent banged on their door for five minutes but no one answered, and then he tells Bryce he isn't surprised because they always miss the early flight. Of course he didn't bother to tell anyone that when he took their reservations, but there you go. So Bryce was looking at a delay on the ground while they stood around and talked about it, and he knew the Bosses were going to be pissed because Tanana was his first stop and he was already dragging. He hated being behind schedule. Plus they had taken all that time in Fairbanks to load the plane for downriver so there would be room to fit the passengers, and now there was no reason for that extra work. It was just one more part of the job that he had no control over, and it drove him crazy. The more he thought about how bad he wanted to leave the Company, the more shit like this just set him over the edge.

"So he was preoccupied when he got back in the air-plane. He was thinking about how pissed he was and his lazy passengers and the screwed-up schedule; he was think-ing about a lot of things that had nothing to do with flying. Bryce's head wasn't in the cockpit when he got back into the plane. He wasn't focused on flying and that would have been okay, heck it would have just another day at work, if nothing went wrong."

"But this wasn't Bryce's day to be lucky," said Frank.

"The way it turned out," said Tony, "it wasn't Bryce's day at all."

"And here we go," said Sam. "Here we go."

"So when the right engine didn't fire right away on the ground, he wasn't really concerned," Scott went on. "He had to crank it again and then again before it finally caught, but that happens, especially with 089. Mostly it was just another thing to annoy him. He was only in the air for a couple of minutes after takeoff though when the engine began to mis-fire. It struggled, tried to regain its rhythm, and then stalled out. We know he did all the things you're supposed to do for a restart: Put the mixture at full rich, the power to idle, the prop to full forward, but still there was no response from the engine. The mags were on, there was fuel in both tanks; there was no obvious reason for the engine to fail. But it just hung there not moving, refusing all attempts at restart, refusing to do anything at all.

"It was just dead," said Scott, "and when you think about it you realize that Bryce had never seen a truly dead engine in the air before. He had never been in this situation, and when the shit was hitting the fan, he froze up. He lost it."

"Decision time," said Sam. "Make it or break it."

"He was up for grabs," said Tony. "Act right, act fast, and you live. The other way, you're a dead man; nothing's going to save you, nothing's going to catch you when you fall."

"So do something," said Frank. "Don't just sit there. Do anything. Why didn't he at least do something?"

"Yeah," said Scott, "seems obvious; just do anything. The deciding vote on his life or death was what Bryce did next, what he did when he knew that engine was lost. He had a problem, a serious problem; hell he lost an engine on takeoff, but still it was recoverable, it was something he was trained to handle. But his mind wandered away from dealing with it and back to that place he had been on the ground. Back to all the things that went wrong on the flight already. And instead of flying the plane, moving past the problem to a solution, he started considering the engine itself and why it failed and what might have caused it.

"He cursed the engine, cursed Maintenance for not fixing it, cursed himself for not paying closer attention to it on the flight from Fairbanks. Mostly, though, he cursed the Company for owning such piece-of-shit airplanes to begin with. He wrapped his brain around emotions instead of focusing on the problem. He didn't notice as the plane began its slow descent to the ground; he took too long to realize that he was not going to get that engine going again and had to land right away. He didn't accept that what he had was a crashing sort of problem, an immediate situation. Instead he fucked around with his time like he had forever to figure out what to do next. While he refused to act, Bryce lost any chance of ever making the airport."

"He lost any chance of making it at all," said Tony.

"Suicide," concluded Frank, "he committed suicide. But I can't believe he killed himself because he was too pissed off to think straight. It doesn't seem possible."

"It could happen," I said. "You can't control where your brain's going to go in a time like that. You can't force it to stay in the right place."

"You can fly the airplane," said Frank. "You can remember to do your job."

"Maybe some guys can't," said Sam. "Maybe this is when they realize they never could."

"You can't catch this in training all the time," said Scott. "Sometimes they get past you. A guy seems like a good pilot, he flies like a good pilot, but who knows really what's going to happen at the 'gone to hell' moment? Who knows what any of us will do until we're there?"

But they all knew that they would make it, and that's why understanding Bryce was so damn hard.

———

It was a rapid-fire time Bryce was living in then; assess, respond, get-your-shit-in-gear kind of time. Everything had to happen quickly because on one engine you have to be flying that airplane every second; if you're on one engine at less than two thousand feet, the only chance you have at making it is if you are only thinking about flying that airplane. There's no room for stray thoughts or questions. You have to be quick and smart and certain. And when you are low and losing altitude and the airport is still a ways off, you have to be thinking about putting the plane down someplace else. You have to, if you want to live.

If you want to live you can't screw up, and Scott knew this. What he didn't know, what he couldn't understand, is why Bryce had forgotten it.

"All the way down, Bryce flew the way you learn in training," said Scott. "He had all the checklists and procedures memorized, but he didn't know how to prepare for the fear, for the chaos. He didn't know how to stay calm in the cockpit and pay attention to what the airplane was telling him. Worst of all, he didn't know when to accept that he couldn't make the landing perfect. He could have put the plane in the trees, could have controlled the crash as much as possible. But to do that he had to give up on making the airport and accept that the plane would be a total loss, and that just wasn't something Bryce was willing to do. So he didn't take his eyes off the airport and radioed one last time that he was over the river and clipping trees but still trying to return to the runway. And that was the last thing he said.

"When he turned back to the village Bryce must have been thinking he could make it," said Scott. "In fact, it must have been all he thought about. He told flight service he might need to ditch, but he never lined the airplane up for anything other than the field. He believed he could make it to the runway, that everything would be fine. He thought he had time to be choosey. He never understood that time was a luxury that belonged to the perfect flights, that it no longer belonged to him. He didn't try to put the plane in the trees, didn't line up for a gravel bar. He never took his eyes off the runway; he never believed it was impossible. Even as the plane was crashing into the Yukon, I bet he thought he could make it," said Scott, "and that was what killed him.

"Bryce was looking right at the river, but he still thought he could make it to the runway," Scott concluded. "He thought there was still a choice that included the airplane. He just forgot how to save himself at the same time. Trying to save the aircraft, he forgot how to save himself."

"All the way down Bryce thought only one thing," said Sam, shaking his head, "and it was everything else that killed him."

"Christ," said Frank, "can you imagine a sadder way to die?"

———————

Or maybe it wasn't like that at all. Maybe he did pay attention; maybe he did work the problem. He still couldn't save it, though, because he worked the wrong problem—he missed what was killing the airplane because he only went after the obvious. And once he found what he was looking for, he stopped looking for anything else.

"This is how it happened," said Sam, and his story was not like Scott's at all. "When Bryce left the village, he had standard configuration for a soft field takeoff, one notch of flaps and the cowl flaps open. He was in the air for just a couple of minutes, though, before the right engine started to miss and then stalled. He ran through the procedure for a lost engine, jumping in his head through the checklist for a restart. To maintain altitude he had to get the flaps up, and so he hit the switch and also closed the cowl flaps. The wing flaps should have both shifted back up, but they didn't because the flap motor failed. Bryce was back to the engine, though, back to working the restart. He didn't double-check the flaps or think about them again. His critical mistake was that he thought the engine was his only problem, and he was dead wrong.

"At about five minutes after departure, we know Bryce radioed Flight Service that he was having a problem and might need to ditch. He had already turned back by then, was trying to make the runway. Even without the right engine, he knew he should have no problem returning to the village; he wasn't carrying a heavy load and the weather was good. He could see the runway clearly; he knew exactly where he needed to go. But what he didn't understand, what he never figured out, was why the plane was losing altitude. It was a struggle to keep it in the air, and it shouldn't have been.

"He knew how to fly the Navajo with one engine. He knew what to expect. The airplane was just not doing what it was supposed to, and Bryce was lost as to what else could be wrong. He got stuck with should-have-been and kept trying to make the airplane show him what he expected. Once he had the dead engine, it blinded him to anything else. He expected the flaps to retract; he needed them to retract, so he didn't even consider that they wouldn't. He kept working the engine, kept trying to fly the plane like it should be flying and didn't notice anything else."

"He never flew the plane he had," said Scott. "He flew the one he expected to see."

"He flew the textbook," said Tony, "and that was all."

"And that's why it wasn't enough," said Frank.

"So how does he save it then?" I asked.

"If he never retracted the flaps, then he wasn't getting back to the field," said Sam. "There was no way he could keep it in air that long in that configuration. So he had to ditch. He had to put it down and save himself, save some of the airplane, but more than anything he had to give up on the engine and the runway."

"Didn't do it," said Tony.

"Didn't even try," said Frank.

"Nope," said Sam, "he got stuck on not understanding why he was falling and instead kept trying to bring that engine back. He was reaching for the wrong answers, the wrong solutions. He should never have even tried a restart on the engine, not on takeoff. There's no room to maneuver that low, especially when you can't hold altitude."

All of us knew that at cruise, one working engine on a twin-engine airplane is plenty to keep you in the air. If you're over five thousand feet you have all the time in the world to decide where to land, but losing an engine on takeoff or during any critical phase of flight demands all of your attention. You have to be thinking of anything and everything that might make it harder for the surviving engine to maintain altitude. You have to be open to every conceivable possibility that will bring your plane down. You don't have the luxury of making mistakes during takeoff; you're too low for that.

"What he should have done was give up on it," said Sam, "accept that his right engine was just dead weight that couldn't help him. It was time to fly single-engine, to land single-engine. It was time to work with what he had left and forget about what was gone.

"Mostly, though, Bryce had to forget about what he personally stood to lose: the airline career, the ticket out of Alaska. He had to just focus on that moment and what was the best thing to do right there."

"But he couldn't let go of his clean record," said Scott. "He liked being that guy too much."

"Put it on the runway with one engine and it's a non-event," agreed Sam. "Put it in the trees and maybe it's your chance at a jet job."

"Put it in the river and it's your life," said Tony.

"Some guys never think that way though," said Frank.

"Idiots," said Tony.

"No," said Scott, "dead guys."

When the plane was pulled out of the river, the Feds were able to study the left wing and engine and see that the flaps were still set for takeoff. They also found that the cowl flaps were open as well. The wing flaps had been stuck on a flight the day before, and the plane never even got off the ground because of it. Maintenance signed the write-up off as "unable to duplicate," though, because in the shop they couldn't find anything broken to fix. There was probably an electrical gremlin in the flap motor somewhere, something that happened quite a bit with aging, beat-to-hell airplanes.

"Bryce knew that morning what happened the day before, and he should have been looking for it to happen again," said Sam. "Whether he did or not we will never know. But that still doesn't explain the cowl flaps. Apparently Bryce never even attempted to close them. So either he tried the wing flaps and the motor failed and he just didn't catch it and then spaced out the cowl flaps, or he spaced out both sets of flaps and never thought about anything other than the engine."

"He saw only one problem," said Scott.

"The obvious problem," said Sam.

"And he never looked anyplace else," said Tony.

Without considering anything else, Bryce lost ten knots of airspeed from the open cowl flaps alone. Combined with the lost engine and raised wing flaps, there was no way the airplane could have maintained altitude; it was impossible.

"Bryce thought he was flying on one engine, but really he was riding a seven-thousand-pound brick out of the sky," said Sam. "He was just a guy holding on for dear life. When it crashed into the river he had no control; he was a passenger, praying for divine intervention."

"I guess God was busy that day," I said.

"God's never there when you're crashing," said Frank.

"Amen," said Tony, who didn't believe in God anyway.

"Wouldn't have mattered if he did show up," said Sam. "Even a miracle couldn't have kept that plane from falling. Only Bryce could do that, and he was too busy crashing to try; he was too busy already dying to do anything like save himself."

And really, there was nothing anyone could add after that.

———•———

For the longest time, Tony was the only one who never cared about the right engine; he called it a red herring. "You want to believe there was something wrong with the engine because then you understand everything else," he said. "But what does it really matter? Even if that engine was blown to hell and back, who really cares? Lose an engine, land the airplane. That's what we do, and we've all done it. We've done it in snowstorms and fog and wind. Bryce had none of that to worry about. Fuck the right engine. It doesn't matter. And it wasn't part of this anyway."

Tony was always certain about things, but his high flight time meant he was allowed to be. He had lost one engine on takeoff flying heavy in the dark in a snowstorm and flown two separate airplanes with the spinners installed incorrectly, leading to engine failure both times (which did make him think for a while that Maintenance was trying to kill him). Tony knew about things going to shit in a second, and he read Bryce's accident as fear and indecision. "He did the wrong thing first, and then he did nothing to fix it. Pilot error," he said. "Doesn't matter about the rest because it was pilot error that killed him.

"*This* is how it happened," Tony said.

"There was never anything wrong with the right engine. It had a rough start, but that wasn't unusual for a Navajo. When he got in the air, Bryce was still worried about it though, wondering why it struggled so much, watching the gauges for anything out of the ordinary. He was expecting more trouble from the right engine, which is why the sudden loud noise on the left side of the airplane took him so much by surprise.

"Air flew through the airplane's cabin. It was like sticking your head out the window while driving down the highway at fifty miles an hour. Immediately he could feel drag affecting the plane. Bryce figured he knew what the problem was and he didn't hesitate; he began shutting down the left engine. He wanted an engine problem. He was expecting one, and just because it was the left side and not the right didn't change anything to him. Now he figured it was just the left engine he should have been worried about all along.

"He had some trouble maintaining altitude, but he could do it. As soon as he had the plane under control, he figured he'd turn back for the airport; and once he landed I bet he was planning to get on the phone and scream at whoever answered. We all know he was sick and tired of flying those airplanes, and he was going to make the Company hear about it."

"His head was in what he was going to do on the ground later," said Scott, "not on how he was going to get there."

"Exactly," agreed Tony. "He was thinking about that conversation, about how much he was going to enjoy blasting Maintenance when he finally realized that nothing had changed in the airplane. The left engine was shut down, but air was still rushing through the cabin and now, without that power, there was enormous drag on the left side of the plane. That's when Bryce knew that he had made a mistake, a huge mistake. There was nothing wrong with the left engine, and shutting it down had only made things worse."

"He compounded the initial problem by creating his own, more serious, secondary problem," said Sam.

"He made another mess," agreed Frank, "and now he had to handle the effects of both of them in order to land."

"Exactly," said Tony. "He had to turn the plane if he wanted to make the airport, and we all know that making the airport was the only thing he wanted to do. The drag on the left side was bad, though, and he was losing serious altitude. He couldn't try restarting the engine and he knew it; he had to turn the plane around, and he had to fly it back the way it was. But his head couldn't leave it alone; he was freaking out over it, over what might have gone wrong. Had he blown out a window or lost part of the fuselage? He had no clue what the real problem was, only that it wasn't an engine problem, but by then he knew that even with two engines he might not be able to pull the plane out of it; there might not be enough power left, period, to salvage that landing. The altimeter was spinning and the ground was rushing up to meet him. And the wind just kept screaming through the cabin."

"He was seeing the same thing again," said Sam, "what he expected and not what was really there."

"Running down a rabbit trail and getting lost," agreed Scott. "Bryce thought he knew what the plane was saying without listening to it."

"First thing he did was wrong, and then he wasted too much time refusing to see how wrong he was," concluded Frank. "After he turned the plane around, the only chance he had was to put it down fast, put it down anywhere."

"But he couldn't do that," I said; "we know that."

"No, he couldn't," said Scott, "but anybody else would have. Shit, anybody else would have loved the excuse to put it down on a gravel bar."

"But it wasn't anybody else flying that day," said Sam. "It was Bryce, and so it had to be Bryce's way."

"Bryce's way killed him," I said.

"Still," said Sam, "it was the only way out for him. By then, the only way out meant Bryce wasn't going to make it."

"Maybe for a second he did consider just putting the plane down," argued Tony. "We're never going to know for sure what he was thinking up there. But the truth is it was going to be a hard landing, a brutal landing, and he had never done anything like that before. He didn't know for sure how to set up for it, and by then the only decision that was still his to make was getting the plane on the runway; that was the place where he could regain control. He figured all he needed to do was hold the plane straight and level through the turn and get to the airport; everything was going to be okay once he got back there."

"But by then of course, there was no way that plane was going to make it back to the runway." said Sam.

"What Bryce never figured out," said Tony, "what he didn't even consider was that the aft door was open. It was the source of the noise, the entry point for all that wind. Having the back door pop open on takeoff happens a lot; it's happened to me a dozen times and to all of you too. It's insignificant really, almost nothing on the list of things that can go wrong during a flight. If he had figured out from the beginning that it was only the door, then all Bryce had to do was land the airplane carefully so that he didn't drag the dropped steps on the runway. But he was preoccupied by potential trouble with the right engine, so when he heard that noise, when it all seemed to go to hell so fast, he just assumed there was trouble with the left engine and he never considered anything else. He forgot to listen to the airplane and instead heard only his own fears. He heard his own worries and nothing else."

When you are making the right choices in the cockpit, you have all the time in the world. After Bryce made the wrong one, he had no time at all. "He flew into the river on one engine with an open door and flaps still set in the takeoff position," said Tony. "Everything he did, and everything he forgot to do, pulled that airplane out of the sky." The Yukon had Bryce when he was still in the air, had him from the first moment the door fell open; he just didn't realize it until the very last second. The poor guy thought he had a chance—until he died, he thought he had a chance. "Pilot error," said Tony, "stupid, fucking, pointless pilot error. He should have saved himself; he *could* have saved himself."

"He shouldn't be dead," said Frank. "End of the story; Bryce shouldn't be dead."

Frank had argued at the accident site, tried to convince the divers to keep looking for the missing engine, tried to make the Feds understand how important it could be in their investigation. It was a losing battle. The Feds were pragmatic, and it wasn't hard to understand why. Several of them knew Bryce and they liked him, but they had seen enough to guess what he had done, and it seemed pretty clear that mistakes had been made. And even from the beginning we all felt that way too, at least a little bit.

Hell, there was only one crash that happened in all the years I lived in Alaska where no one was to blame, and those poor guys had a wing burn off in flight, giving them no chance for survival. That's the kind of bad thing that had to happen to you up there to make other pilots feel sorry for you; you had to be *doomed*. Standing there at the river looking at the wreck, what Frank wanted to know right away though, what we all still wanted to know now, was why Bryce had doomed himself—why, regardless of the problem, he had insisted on heading back for the field.

Everyone at that crash site agreed that there were opportunities for landing the plane before the airport, and no one knew why Bryce didn't at least try for one of them. No one knew why he locked onto the runway and didn't look anywhere else. No one knew why he flew into the river, and the plain truth was that even if we had the right engine, we still weren't going to find the answer to that question. We still weren't going to know what was in Bryce's head that day that made the impossible his best and only choice.

We all hated knowing that, and sometimes, because of it, we hated Bryce too.

The older I get, the more I try to understand what Bryce was thinking before he died. There isn't much you can do about the stuff that jumps into your head sometimes, the sometimes less-than-charitable thoughts about a dead friend. Maybe he didn't want to worry about his career but couldn't shake the thought that a crash landing would ruin his future, trapping him at the Company forever. Or maybe even if Bryce wanted to put the plane down on a gravel bar, his head just kept telling him to go a little farther, try a little longer for the runway. And when he finally realized that he couldn't make it, there was no other option than the river.

Maybe in the end he believed he could ditch it in the Yukon and still survive. But the odds are slim on that choice. That river is not a landing kind of river. Maybe Bryce thought he would be the one to beat it, or maybe he just didn't realize that the river was never an option and fooled himself into thinking it was.

Maybe he fooled all of us.

So this is how it happened: Something broke; something malfunctioned and Bryce tried to fix it and couldn't or did the right thing too slowly or the wrong thing too many times, or maybe the piece-of-shit airplane he was flying finally proved itself to truly be a complete piece of shit and too many things broke at once for anyone to save, no matter how good or fast or smart they were; and because of some of this or all of it, or maybe even none of it, he crashed the airplane. How his accident happened is a mystery, a puzzle with too many missing pieces to ever clearly see. Maybe he was sick or tired or angry. Maybe his judgment was clouded. Maybe a thousand things we haven't even considered, things we will never know, affected his decisions that morning. Or maybe he really did everything right and the airport was attainable; it was fine, and then something failed before he knew it or without him being able to know, and he never meant to go into the river; he truly believed he had it under control until it was too late. Anything is possible with this crash, anything. The only certainty is that something bad happened to Bryce, and that is all we will ever have from that day on the Yukon River. Sometimes that's all you get in Alaska though; it tells you nothing, but it's all you get.

What we know for sure is that Bryce took off, and five minutes later he was dead. Everything else is just what we think, what we talk about, what we sometimes believe. It could all be true, or at least partly true; I don't know. It could just as easily be a bunch of lies as well. We play a game when we talk about Bryce, a game of what might have been. No one ever agrees when we finish; no one changes his mind. It's just a game of frustration, endless frustration. But what else are we ever going to do?

The final official determination on Bryce Donovan's accident was "Probable Cause Unknown," and the Feds told us that was a gift, really. Not knowing for sure was a gift.

17
Looking for Ben Eielson

Ben Eielson's crash in 1929 was the kind of tragedy that allowed hyperbole to overwhelm the facts. Only a matter of days after the wreckage was found, he was anointed as the pilot who sacrificed himself for the good of Alaska, for the selfless benefit *of all Alaskans.* It was a death tailor made for mythmakers everywhere, and nothing will ever change it.

Eielson went missing on November 9, nearly two months after the search for Russ Merrill had begun. After his miraculous survival on the Barrow flight the year before, it had been hard—if not impossible—for everyone to believe that Merrill would not be found alive again. Pilots converged on Anchorage in September as soon as Merrill was reported overdue and began flying different routes every day in search not only of a crash site but also any evidence that he had even been seen. Eielson was part of the effort until he was pulled away by a fifty-thousand-dollar contract his airline signed with the Swenson Fur Trading Company (which would be worth about $636,000 today).

The Swensons had a million-dollar cargo and fifteen employees on the *Nanuk,* which was stuck in the ice near North Cape, Siberia. Concerned that their value would plummet if competitors made it to the showrooms before them, the Swensons contracted Alaskan Airways to transport the six tons of furs to Fairbanks. Eielson was one of two pilots sent to the small village of Teller on Alaska's west coast to fulfill the contract. He was on his second trip to the ship with his mechanic, Earl Borland, when their plane disappeared.

One week after Eielson and Borland disappeared, the *Fairbanks Daily News-Miner* reported they were missing. The second Alaska Airways pilot, Frank Dorbandt, wired the newspaper that he believed "Eielson is down in some lagoon in Siberia in the storm. Eielson has many days rations, a sleeping bag and a primus stove." Dorbandt had departed just ahead of Eielson but returned due to the weather and had been unable to take off since. In the November 16 article, however, he was certain that Eielson was alive: "Dorbandt said that Olaf Swenson, aboard the *Nanuk,* wired: 'Eight days ago just as it was getting dark with bad visibility Eielson circled around a native's house twice about 60 miles from here, but did not land.'"

Dorbandt's aircraft was damaged, but he intended to continue searching as soon as he was able. Other pilots were also planning to travel north when the weather permitted. It was all sobering news; first Merrill and now Eielson. And yet after little more than a week, it is important to note that while Eielson was lost to Dorbandt and others, he was not yet *missing*.

There were many reasons to not initially assume the worst, starting with the fact that this was, after all, Ben Eielson. If anyone could land on the tundra and survive for weeks it was he. And there was also Merrill and Wien's Barrow flight to remember. Alaskan pilots were masters at performing miracles; they made it look easy.

"It is not a time for hasty conclusions," noted an *Anchorage Daily Times* editorial in late September concerning Merrill, "for, in the absence of proof that serious mishap has befallen the missing airman, there is the chance that he will yet be found; in the face of all the good luck that has brought him through his earlier narrow squeezes in Alaska, it is hard to believe now that he has not had another lucky escape from disaster."

And yet, by the time the search began in earnest for Eielson and Borland, by the time Joe Crosson and Harold Gillam, Matt Nieminen, Harvey Barnhill, and Ed Young were all joining Frank Dorbandt to crisscross the skies over eastern Siberia, the realization that Russ Merrill was gone forever was beginning to sink in. "Piece of Torn Fabric Brought to Anchorage: Part of Missing Ship" ran the headline in the Anchorage newspaper on October 21. The fabric was found on the beach in Tyonek, a small village on the west shore of Cook Inlet. Coupled with reports from village residents concerning a strange object seen drifting in the distance back in September, Joe Crosson concluded that Merrill must have been forced down not long after leaving Anchorage. A storm the next day would have swept him out to sea before the regular tides could carry him to land. He was, literally, completely and permanently, lost. Merrill's disappearance, reported in Juneau's *Daily Alaska Empire* in late January, "remains one of the mysteries of air navigation in Alaska."

When Jean Potter wrote her book on Alaska's aviation history, *The Flying North,* in 1942, she spoke with the men who searched for Eielson. The manager of the Teller Road House told her, "Never have I seen so much ice, snow, wind, and fog." Potter reported that the temperature that winter dropped to forty below and "repeated seventy-mile gales swept between the two continents." Joe Crosson was the first to arrive, but it made no difference; the weather allowed little flying, and waiting on the weather soon became the most significant part of the rescue.

The official historic weather data from Nome (about fifty-five miles to the south) is still on the shelves of the library at the Geophysical Institute at the University of Alaska, Fairbanks. When I went there as a grad student to see the original records, the librarian was surprised by my request. She asked me to leave my backpack on the floor by the front desk and made it clear the photocopier would be off-limits. I was ushered into a small back office where decades of state weather records lined the shelves. The librarian pointed out the Nome notebooks for the years 1928, 1929, and 1930; then, with a long backward glance and reminder to treat the books with extreme care, she left me to my research. She did not, however, close the door.

The heavy cardboard covers were warped and stained with age, but the handwriting was still clear. Through the month of November 1929, there were twenty-three days of dense fog and eighteen of snow. The temperatures hovered in the low twenties with northeast winds, and on the tenth a squall was reported. This was the storm that had grounded Frank Dorbandt. In Nome the weather observer could not know that Eielson was overdue as the wind blew through; but in the days to come, as storms covered the peninsula, word would have reached everyone that he had not returned. According to Potter, the *Nanuk* reported similar conditions: "Ceiling and visibility nil nil" and "High winds." The pilots tried to take off, over and over they tried, but little flying was accomplished. "Time after time a fur-bundled pilot took off from the frozen runway to scout the sky, only to return with bad news: Bering Strait was impassable."

The delays dragged on until one month and then a second went by, and slowly everyone began to accept there was no miracle big enough for Eielson and Borland. When Joe Crosson finally saw a piece of metal sticking out of the snow on January 19, he and Harold Gillam landed and, even without the bodies, they knew. They knew that any faint and foolish hope was gone forever. The aircraft, ninety miles southeast of the *Nanuk,* was broken in two, the right wing two hundred feet from the cabin and the engine torn loose and buried more than one hundred feet away. Crosson determined that they hit the ground at what he later termed "flying speed." No one could have survived.

Because of the heavy snow that had fallen since the accident, it took more than three weeks of steady digging by a combined group of Russians and Americans before Eielson's and Borland's bodies were recovered. Then there was a further delay until the weather was good enough to fly them back to Alaska. Finally they arrived in Fairbanks, where Ole Eielson was waiting to take his son home to North Dakota.

"As long as the search continued, there was the chance they had escaped disaster; the finding of the wrecked ship in such a desolate region, with temperatures far below zero, could mean only one thing. But with the sorrow there will come, at least, an end to the suspense, relief from the long period of uncertainty and perhaps, as the father of Colonel Eielson puts it, the bereft will find even a measure of comfort now in the confirmation of that which they long suspect."

So said the editors at the *Anchorage Daily Times,* but I wondered if there was any comfort to be found for Ole Eielson, who now would visit both his wife and son at the same cemetery. Is there ever any comfort to be found when someone you love goes away forever? What must it be like for so many families, time and again, to bury young men who were chasing a dream only to lose it in such a devastating and violent manner?

In Alaskan history, in aviation history, Eielson didn't die on the job, he died for a cause. He was the pilot who flew over the North Pole and Antarctica; he was always about something more than just the business of flying. Accepting that makes it no surprise that his economic reasons for taking off that final day from Teller in such poor weather were ignored. The articles following the discovery of the wreckage all focused on the ideal of a great man, and great men do not make mistakes because they are thinking about the financial bottom line. Great men are never preoccupied or careless. Almost by themselves, stories formed about the dead hero everyone needed Eielson to be: the bush pilot who crashed on a mercy mission.

From Antarctica the explorer George Wilkins issued a statement that read in part, "Eielson and I together had seen, in the North and in the South, more than half a million square miles of the earth's surface that no other human eyes had seen." He could not believe that his friend would have died for anything less than a lifesaving mission. "Eielson will live in exploring history as long as men fly over the earth. Typically, he died while trying to effect the rescue of a fur-trading ship caught in the ice."

Everybody loved that heroic story. It was what they longed to read because it wasn't about what really happened in Teller. It was about who they collectively believed a man like Ben Eielson *must have been.*

The myth of Ben Eielson's death became the grand story of all of Alaska's aviation pioneers, and it is still repeated, even today, whenever Eielson's name is mentioned. He was a hero; he was always a hero, and so was Russ Merrill and so was Ralph Wien and so was Harold Gillam. Ben Eielson was going to die for greatness. He had to, it was the only thing everyone else could live with.

———•———

It was years after I studied Eielson in school that I came across a quote from England's former Lord Chancellor, Lord Henry Brougham, writing about Victorian explorers who went to the North. "They cannot help it," he explained. "It is in the blood."

Is that what we have to believe, really? Does it have to be something as big as that—something innately biological? A "noble obsession"? What if it's more pedestrian, if those nineteenth-century explorers were just bored or desperate for cash or eager to meet different people and see different places? Maybe they were leaving bad romances and parents who never understood and expectations they could never fulfill. Maybe they just wanted something else and home could not give them that; it couldn't because home was always the same, and sometimes that alone is the only reason you need to leave.

Maybe Ben Eielson went to Alaska because he liked flying, and even though he tried he couldn't find a way to make that happen in the Lower 48. Alaska at least was some place that wasn't North Dakota, that wasn't full of everyone he knew and everywhere he had been. And then, somewhere in the middle of the adventure and the friendships, he found himself—he found a place that was truly and only his.

Alaska embraced Ben Eielson; it made him a legend. Without it he might have disappeared far sooner, vanished as one more of those dreamers who tried to find himself and missed somehow. No one would know about all of his hopes for changing the aviation landscape, for making Alaska the center of the commercial airline world, if he hadn't gone north.

No one would know who he was other than the Eielson family from Hatton, North Dakota, and that would have had to be enough for him; that would have been all he ever was. Ben chose something different, which hopefully, before he died, his family understood.

When I went to my grandmother's funeral five years after my father died, I spent an afternoon in the house with my grandfather. My grandparents moved there soon after they married; it had been their home for more than sixty years. We wandered through the house as he shared memories, and then he walked across the room and picked up a framed document hanging on a nail in my father's old attic bedroom. "You should have this," he said, handing it to me. It was a certificate for excellent penmanship from Holy Family School awarded to my father in the second grade. "Bobby was always a good student," he said. "We were so proud of him."

My father left home when he was seventeen, but his parents still clung for decades to small moments from his childhood. I wonder still what Ben Eielson's father held onto while his son was far away, what stayed behind in North Dakota long after Ben was gone, and what was waiting when he finally came home.

18

One Hundred Crash Stories

One day, one day like any other at the Company, there was a little girl who came in with her mother and siblings for a scheduled flight to Nulato. They were a well-behaved group of kids. They talked to one another and the people who came to see them off. They were going to the village to visit family. They talked about fishing and playing with cousins. All except the one little girl. She sat by herself, against the wall, away from the crowd with her head lowered, studying the carpet. Everyone spoke to her as they walked by, but she didn't look up.

There was something I saw out of the corner of my eye, something about her that was not quite right. She looked down, she looked away; she fixated on the wall behind her, the door to her left, ignoring me and everyone else. There was something she didn't want anyone to see.

Frank came out and finished his paperwork, calling out to the family while he worked on it, joking with the mother. He rarely flew the afternoon flight, but the Bosses said this was how it needed to be when they saw the reservation sheets a few days before. This was going to be Frank's flight. And he didn't argue when they scheduled him. It had to be Frank or Tony, said the Bosses, and Frank was happy to take it. This flight was special.

No one said why though.

He talked to the mother as he put together the flight tin and crammed in the manifest and freight slips. He asked the kids how they were doing in school and they chattered back, telling him it was fun or stupid or boring. It was clear that he knew this family. The little girl stood up and walked out beside him.

She wore a mask. A fabric mask that looked like a face, enough to fool you for a minute, but it was a mask nevertheless. She also had a pink butterfly barrette in her hair that matched her shirt. When she sat in the waiting room, she had swung her legs back and forth, small movements, cautious swings. This flight was special because of her.

"It still freaks me out when I see them," said Scott, coming up beside me at the window after they left. We could see the family walking out to the ramp. "The whole thing is just so sad."

"What happened to them?"

"They crashed," he said. "Killed the father and the youngest kid and burned the rest of them. The one girl got it pretty bad. That's why she's covered. Those kids hate to fly; I don't know why their mother still makes them do it; I don't know how she can do it," he said, turning away.

"Tony was down there working in Galena when it happened. You should ask him about it. The weather was dogshit, and the competition pretty much flew it into the river, bounced out, hit some trees. The whole thing burned. The father got out, but he went back for the baby. Went back and then they couldn't get either one of them out. There was another passenger onboard who died too."

The family only flew in the summer now, only on clear days, only with Frank or Tony, pilots they knew from before. They never flew with the competition, never on a day with a cloud in the sky.

"How long has she had the mask?"

"It's been a couple of years at least," Scott said. "We never see her without it, but it'll come off someday. She was the last one out alive, you know, before her father went back. I guess that makes her lucky."

"But not really," I said.

"No," he agreed. "Not really."

Years later there are many things about the Company I have forgotten. There were so many passengers, so many pilots, so many stories. But the little girl is still there, out of the corner of my eye, as she was that first time, only nine or ten years old, still living that crash because she had to, because her face wouldn't let her move on.

I will never know how any of them were able to fly again.

I feel like a thief when I write about her, borrowing her story, stealing her crash, making it part of my education as much as it was her life. I wonder now if I stood at the window memorizing her face because I was thinking, maybe, someday, I will understand better why she matters to me and I'll want to remember her perfectly; I'll want to see those white sandals and that barrette again. I'll want to see that mask ten years later just as clearly as I see it now. I want to make sure I get it right for when I need to write it later.

Do all writers think that way?

———•———

It was pilot error, of course. Tony told me later that flight was the only one out of Galena all day. He was cooling his heels, reading the paper, planning to hit the NCO Club at the base with everyone else, when they collectively agreed to bag it and give up on flying. When the Navajo took off, all the other pilots shook their heads. The pilot had obviously caved to Fairbanks, promised to go take a look when it was obvious he wasn't going to get anywhere.

"There was nothing to see," said Tony, shaking his head. "But he was a newbie and either had something to prove or didn't know how to say no yet."

"Nobody who knew anything was flying that day."

After stopping in Nulato, just twenty minutes downriver, the Navajo was overdue to nearby Kaltag a short time later; calls started coming in from downriver asking pilots to look for them, but no one could get anywhere. The state Fish and Wildlife pilot had a plane on floats and decided to try to step-taxi, but he couldn't even do that. A little while later the pilot made it to the village on foot and they put boats in the water. They got the survivors up to Galena and brought the bodies out later.

"You were still young and crazy then," I said. "Why didn't you try downriver like he did?"

"Because I got all of my stupid out of the way in Bethel," said Tony. "Honestly," he added, "I don't know why any of them went on that flight. The pilot might have been new but the passengers weren't—they lived down there; they knew what was good weather and what wasn't. If nobody else is flying that day, what makes you go with the only idiot who will? It never made any sense to me why the adults went on that flight, any of them. Never made any sense at all."

"But now they fly with you," I said to him, "just you and Frank."

He would have liked to say it was because he was good, but we both knew it was mostly because they had to trust somebody. If they wanted to go back to the village where they were born, where everyone they cared about was waiting to see them, then they had to fly with somebody. They chose Frank and Tony because the one thing everyone knew about the two of them was that nobody was ever going to get them to do anything they didn't want to do.

The mother had learned that when you can't trust yourself to make the right decision, then you need to fly with a pilot who will.

"Does she say anything?" I ask Tony. "The little girl?"

"Sure," he says. "She'll tell you about school and fighting with her sisters and going to see her grandparents. Nothing about being nervous though and nothing about that flight."

"What do you think she's thinking up there when you fly?"

"That it can never be clear enough, I imagine. And that the river is always closer than you think."

"Close enough to reach out and grab," I said.

"Got them didn't it?" he said. "Got them before they even knew it was there."

———

I never saw her without the mask. They flew with us about a half dozen times while I was at the Company, always calling a couple of weeks ahead, always making sure to ask that the Bosses knew they were scheduled; always hinting that there needed to be a certain pilot or certain weather. They never flew on the competition. The rumor was they could have owned that company if they wanted to and it was a threatened lawsuit that bought the mother a new SUV. But what did that matter when you thought about the father running into a burning plane after his kids, going back until there was only the last one, the smallest one, the one that fell far away from them when they crashed, the one he couldn't find.

Of course we always scheduled them with Frank or Tony.

I found the official accident report when I was researching pilot error accidents in grad school. It was short, like most of the older reports, just a few sentences typed online from the original, which was filed who knows where. "The pilot reported that the #2 engine began to lose power as he was flying under a low overcast and about 500 ft. above a river. Subsequently, the airplane descended and the fuselage and left propeller contacted the water. With these problems and decreasing visibility ahead, the pilot elected to make a 180-degree turn. He said that about midway through the turn, the #2 engine lost all power. The airplane then crashed into trees and was destroyed by post-impact fire. No reason was found for either engine to lose power before water or tree contact."

"I saw the props when they brought the plane out; both of them were bent back, both of them hit the water while they were spinning. He lost power, all right," said Tony. "After the left engine hit the water.

"He put it into the river because he couldn't see a damn thing, and then he yanked up, hit full power on the right engine, and tried to turn around and rolled it. The plane was upside-down in the trees when it burned. He fucking flipped it because he panicked and couldn't see where he was going and didn't know what he was doing."

"The clouds were down to the water," I said.

"The clouds are down to the water a lot," said Tony.

"His whole story was a lie," I said. "Do you think he believed it?"

"Do you think I care?" he asked.

———————

One story for the pilot, one for the Company who sent him, one for the pilots who decided not to go. One story for the passenger flying alone who didn't make it—a young guy on the way home, jumping the only flight that would try. One for the father in the last moment when he tried to save his baby boy, one for the mother who saw him go back in, one for each of the daughters who lay burned and bleeding on the side of the river.

One for the little girl who still couldn't leave the crash behind because it wouldn't leave her.

The Feds had the official story: "Probable Cause: Failure of the pilot to maintain adequate altitude after becoming distracted with an engine problem. Factors related to the accident were: loss of power in the #2 engine for an unknown reason and the low overcast condition."

"He killed them because he was stupid," said Tony. "That's my story."

Did I know when I saw her that I wouldn't forget her? She never spoke to me. The other girls did, but she was shy. You could forget the crash with the other girls but not her. And the crash was what I thought about when I saw her. I never understood how they could get on our Navajos and see the same door close, watch the same view from those same windows, wait for that river to lead them back to the village.

"Is anybody's story better than the rest?"

"I only know it second-hand," said Scott. "I only know Tony's story."

"His is just as good as anyone else who was there," said Frank. "Anybody else who had half a brain and knew not to fly."

"It's the one where the pilot didn't crash," said Tony.

"Maybe that's why they like to fly with you," I said, "looking for a new ending."

"Happily ever fucking after," said Frank. "Even when you didn't have one, everyone still wants it."

———•———

She always had a barrette in her hair, and when she looked at you, there was no way not to stare at the mask. The plane crashed while she looked at you; it crashed and her family fell to pieces. She walked out the door to get on one of our Navajos and I watched her burn. That was the story that mattered because it wasn't over yet. Until the crash let her go, it wasn't ever going to end. So that's the one I wrote about even though it's the shortest one I ever heard. It's the one I'm still writing almost twenty years after it happened. Somewhere now she is long past barrettes and swinging her feet, and maybe the scars have faded away; maybe she isn't that little girl anymore.

Maybe where she is now, no one knows she ever was.

19

Our Missing Aviator

What is there to say when a flier drops out of sight as completely as Pilot Merrill appears to have done? The Times *gropes for words but cannot find them. It is not a time for hasty conclusions, for, in the absence of proof that serious mishap has befallen the missing airman, there is the chance that he will yet be found; in the face of all the good luck that has brought him through his earlier narrow squeezes in Alaska, it is hard to believe now that he has not had another lucky escape from disaster.*
—Anchorage Daily Times, *September 28, 1929*

He was going home. Sitting in Anchorage International, waiting for the jet, Sam considered what his family would notice first: the dark circles under his eyes that seemed to go on forever, the lost weight, the lost hair. So many pieces of who he used to be were missing now, strewn across the Arctic. He could not find his camera, his favorite baseball cap, the pen that wrote at twenty below. He lost a Notre Dame sweatshirt, a copy of *The Martian Chronicles*, and the names of a dozen old friends.

Sam knew his family would notice that he was different, but how could he explain that fourteen hundred hours of flight time a year meant ten thousand chances for some sudden moment of anxiety, for his heart to skip a beat or the air to seize in his lungs. There were so many chances for something to go wrong. The things he could not control seemed lately to be everywhere. He was in trouble, big trouble, and he knew it. He told the Bosses he had to leave Barrow for a while; he had to leave Alaska. It was way past time to get Outside and figure some things out. Sometimes he looked down and saw his hands were shaking and did not know why, or how to make them stop.

It was time to go home.

Pilot Russell H. Merrill, who hopped off for the Kuskokwim River a week ago yesterday, in the Travelair cabin plane of the Alaskan Airways, appears to have disappeared completely, the search for him, which has been in progress since Saturday, having failed to find any trace of the missing pilot or his plane.
—Anchorage Daily Times, *September 24, 1929*

After a few years of flying up North, Sam had begun to wonder if anyone really had accidents. Was it possible for so many apparently decent pilots to repeat each other's fatal mistakes again and again? Five dead guys he knew one year, ten the next. Were they all trying to kill themselves or just suffering from some collective form of suicidal stupidity? Did Alaska attract only those pilots who had to defy death in order to consider themselves any good?

God, were all of them just idiots, including him?

Could it be that simple?

And there was the problem with his hands. Lately they had started shaking when he was tying down a load or filling out a manifest. He found himself looking down at fingers that belonged to someone else, at a wrist that had to hold on to his hand for dear life. Watching them bounce across the yoke one day, Sam thought maybe it was time to go, time to go back to what he knew, back to where he came from. The problem was that someone else's family lived at the top of his old driveway now, some other boy hung model airplanes in his childhood bedroom. His parents told him to come and see the new place, come and stay in the guest room. Come and *visit* they told him on the telephone. And Sam knew his crash had already begun.

> *Undiscouraged by failure to find any trace of Pilot Russell [sic] H. Merrill on previous flights, the search for the missing Anchorage airman was resumed today with increased determination and with additional facilities for carrying on the hunt, under the direction of Col. C. B. Eielson, head of the Alaska Airway.*
> —Anchorage Daily Times, *September 28, 1929*

When he thought about it, Sam was amazed by how places that seemed so exotic and strange when he first came to Alaska now rolled off his tongue without a second thought.

He was surprised by how he said them so easily, reciting them to his curious mother and father on those early visits home like a bored schoolboy rather than stumbling and struggling as he did in the weeks after he arrived. He knew them all now, better than he had ever known anyplace.

Anaktuvuk is cold, he told his parents, and so are Allakaket and Chalkyitsik and Venetie and Galena and Koyukuk and Nulato and Kaltag. The snow blows like shattered glass in Kotzebue and Selawik and Noorvik and Nome and Moses Point. The wind is everywhere in the Y-K Delta. It sweeps across places like Bethel and Kongiganak and Eek and Scammon Bay and Tuntutuliak and Chevak with a force that is so freezing and so stupefying that it cannot be described; it has to be lived. It rains and it fogs in Goodnews and Platinum, blinding you in a grayness that you can taste and touch. And Barrow, everyone asked him later; you've lived there for a year now, what is Barrow like?

This was where Sam paused, where he had to think. How could he tell them something distinctive, something more? Barrow is cold, it's covered in snow; it's where the wind is born. It's an all-encompassing barrenness, an emptiness that somehow includes all the villages that surround it to the west, places like Wainwright and Point Lay and Atqasuk, and also the ones to the east, Nuiqsut and Deadhorse and Barter Island. It's 312 miles north of the Arctic Circle, he could say, the place the Inupiat camped in over a thousand years ago but did not exist officially until Frederick Beechey discovered it for England in 1826 and named it for a guy no one in Alaska had ever heard of. It's the kind of place the schools forget to mention and the history books could care less about. How do you explain a country called Barrow? How do you make them understand?

Does anyone really care what he knows about it anyway?

It's the end of the world, Sam could tell them, and I've seen it. It's the corner of an ocean that goes on to a place like the Amazon, like the Sahara. It goes to a darkness that doesn't live on maps or memories. It is *away,* far far away. It is forever far away.

"What is Barrow like?" his parents ask him now, now that he has run back to them, and he still doesn't know how to answer. Can he tell them the truth while he's sitting at their kitchen table, drinking orange juice from a Disney World souvenir cup staring at a row of sunflower placemats? Can they understand in Cincinnati, Ohio, what it is like thousands of miles away?

Could anyone?

"It's cold," he says. "It's just what you'd expect, but colder."

And everybody laughs in his mother's yellow kitchen and takes another drink from their mugs of coffee, and Sam drops a napkin down under his chair so he can bend down to pick it up and no one will see his hands are shaking, no one will ask him if he is all right. *Barrow is where I died,* he thinks to himself; *it's the place where they buried me.* And he stays under the table a little while longer, listening to his family laughing above him, laughing about what happens in the cold. Laughing about what they could not possibly ever understand.

Col. C. B. Eielson, head of the air transportation com-
pany, who left Anchorage Saturday in the company's
Waco ship, accompanied by Alonzo Cope, mechanic,
returned to the Anchorage airport this morning. They
landed on a river bar at Sleitmute [sic] and learned
that Pilot Merrill had not been there; they then pushed
on to Akiak, Bethel and to Nyak, the camp of the Bear
Creek Gold Dredging company, where Merrill was
to have delivered a piece of machinery. He had not
reported at any of those places.
—Anchorage Daily Times, *September 24, 1929*

His parents always want to know more about his job.
"What is a typical workday like?" they ask. Sam doesn't
know how to put it into words, how to describe the repeti-
tion, all the flying that is relentlessly the same yet somehow
never typical. When he thought about it, considered it, the
job managed to make some kind of distorted sense, but he
knew it would sound ridiculous to them.

What was flying in Alaska like?

It was not showing up at work the same time every day,
or sitting in the same seat, or seeing the same people. There
was no office, no desk, and no chair waiting for him. Instead
he waited each morning for the flight to reveal itself, for
the Bosses to tell him what part of the plan had changed
overnight, for the weather to surprise them, for airplanes to
break down, for copilots to show up at the last minute. Sam
flew different types of aircraft to different places in different directions. He flew packages in odd-shaped boxes, living creatures and carcasses, caskets and coffins, the sick and

the dying; weeping mourners and wild school children on field trips hundreds of miles away. He never knew anything about his day until it had already started to spin around him. Sometimes that was a wonderful thing and he loved it, but only sometimes.

"It's just flying," he says to his parents, "like driving a bus in the sky."

And his brother laughs from across the table and says again how lucky Sam is to sit on his butt all day and not have to work for a living. His brother shakes his head over Sam's paycheck and flight bag and logbooks. And his parents say, "It's not always easy; sometimes flying can be tough." But his brother doesn't believe it, has never believed it. He stands in the corner of the kitchen and makes a joke about pilots never getting their hands dirty, and Sam thinks family is where you should not have to explain who you are, where they already know you, where they know you best. And he hears his parents asking him to show his hands, laughing about how clean they are, unscarred and unblemished. They are kidding him; it is all a joke. But if they already know the punch line, why do they keep saying it every time he comes home, and why do they always want to check his hands?

Why won't they leave him alone?

Sam turns around and sees that his brother has left the room. Now that the old reliable joke has been told, he has no interest in staying.

The region between Anchorage and Lake Chackacham-
ina has been searched four times, twice by Col. Eielson
and twice by Pilot Joe Crosson, who made a flight as

far as the mountains yesterday with the company's small open plane, equipped with pontoons. The weather was such that he could not get through to the lake, but he made a close search of the route as far as he could go. There are only one or two small lakes between the inlet and Lake Chackachamina, on the route through the mountains, but there are many lakes on the west side of the mountains, toward the Kuskokwim. Every one was closely scanned, the airmen flying low over them to get a closer look.

—Anchorage Daily Times, *September 24, 1929*

Sam had hundreds of photos of the places he flew in and out of, pictures of runways and villages, people coming to meet the plane on their snow machines and four-wheelers. In his parents' house, their new house, he looked at the pictures again, studied them, and tried to understand how these places he knew so well could still seem alien, like remote cloud cities on distant planets. He could visit them forever but still be a foreigner, always an Outsider.

Like he was that day in Kaktovik.

Kaktovik was east of Barrow and the oil rigs of the North Slope, east of everything that made a sprawling metal monster like Deadhorse possible. It was on tiny Barter Island, just off the coast, out in the Arctic Ocean. It was a place of seal hunts and polar bears and the celebration of slaughtered whales. Even though they depended on oil money to give them television and flush toilets, the Inupiat in Kaktovik still managed to live on a different time plane. They brushed up against the twentieth century when it was convenient, when the airplanes came with mail and freight, when the government men came and went from Barter's radar station, when the submarines eased up through the ice to stare at them then slid back under, demanding to be forgotten. But still a large part of Kaktovik resisted what everyone else seemed destined to embrace. "A lot of them don't even speak English up there," Sam told his parents. "They speak something older, something that sounds like a language you never heard before; something *other*." When he flew into Kaktovik to carry passengers to funerals or celebrations, the elders would look at him and shake their heads. They did not know his language, did not want his world. He was just another doomed explorer, and they were not interested in his kind of discovery.

Six months before he left Alaska, there had been a flight to Kaktovik. Sam thought endlessly about it, reconsidered all the decisions over and over again, studied each moment that he could remember and dwelled on all those that were lost to his exhausted memory. The numbers, the distances, were things he was familiar with, calculations he had done a hundred times before. They were easy to replicate, but they always made things difficult.

You couldn't argue with the numbers, couldn't make them lie for you. The numbers had to be physically changed, altered, forced to provide a different conclusion. The numbers were either truth or manipulation. And while Sam knew dozens of ways in which a load manifest or flight log could be transformed, he was unwilling to take a chance with his fuel, especially flying in this particular dark emptiness. The Bosses knew this, but they pushed him anyway. Pushed him to fly heavier and longer, faster and lower. Whatever he had to do in order to get the job done, they wanted. The Bosses always wanted more.

Mrs. Merrill, wife of the missing pilot, joined the search late yesterday afternoon, making a three-hour flight in the Waco plane, piloted by Joe Crosson and accompanied also by Mechanician [sic] Alonzo Cope. They took off from the local airport at 4 o'clock and returned at 7 o'clock, making a landing in the dark. The country was closely scanned for many miles around and the flight extended to the Stillman camp in the Rainy Pass district, to make certain that Pilot Merrill had not altered his course after taking off from Anchorage. A note was dropped to the big game hunters, inquiring if the missing pilot had been seen there since the early afternoon of September 16, and the answer was that he had not.
—Anchorage Daily Times, *September 26, 1929*

From Barrow to Deadhorse was such a common run that Sam flew it that day almost without thinking. It was easy to fuel, easy to come and go while he was still empty of passengers and cargo. But then he flew on to Kaktovik to the true beginning of his charter, and so very quickly his flight fell apart.

There were nine adults and three children waiting for him at the airport, twelve passengers for a plane that legally carried nine. Sam knew the children were over the age of two; all of them should have been in separate seats on their own. But no one on the plane or at the airport spoke English, or they pretended they didn't anyway. Modern America was suddenly absent from his world, and Sam found himself with a group of passengers unwilling to negotiate. They looked straight at him from deep in the pages of a dusty leather-bound book on the Arctic, and Sam understood that they could wait forever. He could ask the same questions again and again and only hear the same silence in return. No one was getting off that plane.

So he was stuck and the numbers would show excessive ground time; they would show a delay and a late arrival in Aklavik. He would have to explain himself to the Company, justify his decisions. He could not sit in Kaktovik and wait for the centuries to finally collide. He had the numbers to consider. So he took them all, took all their baggage, took everything they wanted, and he flew out of Kaktovik. He flew away in the dark and the cold following the disappearing coast to Inuvik, looking for Canadian Customs, reaching for Aklavik. He was trying to make up for lost time, trying to catch the schedule. He was trying to do the impossible.

The mystery surrounding the disappearance of Pilot R. H. Merrill on the evening of September 16, following his departure from Anchorage for the Kuskokwim district in the Travelair cabin plane of the Alaskan Airways, is believed to have been solved by the finding of a piece of torn fabric on the beach of Tyonek, government Indian reservation on the west side of Cook inlet. The tattered and cut section of cloth, about a yard in length, has been positively identified by Mechanician [sic] Alonzo Cope as part of the covering of the tail

piece of the missing plane and the finding of it on the beach is regarded as positive evidence that the plane was forced down and lost in the inlet.
—Anchorage Daily Times, *October 21, 1929*

When he was tired Sam did stupid things. He flew rushed and lazy at the same time, eager to be done with the flight but gripped in a lassitude that made the seat seem so comfortable and his coat so very warm. He failed to check things, to notice things. He eased in and out of altitudes; drifted from one course heading to another, let the wind drag him along to places he should not be. He allowed himself to make mistakes, forgave himself too quickly for errors of precision and control. He read the instruments but failed to see the necessary patterns they were designed to reveal.

More and more his focus narrowed until he lost himself in the completion of fewer and fewer tasks. He could fly straight but not true, could maintain altitude but not without drift. He did not pay adequate attention to the task at hand, could not pay adequate attention. And because he was tired he realized none of this, which meant, really, he should not be flying the airplane at all.

And yet there he was at seven thousand feet between Aklavik and Barrow, finally on the way back. There he was all alone, the passengers safely at their destination, staring mindlessly out the window looking for stars, looking for light. His head was in a dozen different places, none of them in the cockpit. Alone in the night with thoughts he did not have the time for, Sam didn't notice what the gauges said— or that his hands were beginning to shake.

From the information obtained, it is believed by the searchers that Pilot Merrill was forced down in the inlet shortly after he hopped off from Anchorage and that his ship had been adrift all night when it was sighted by the Tyonek natives. The appearance of the piece of fabric found on the beach encourages the belief that it was used by Pilot Merrill as a sail or in an effort to make a raft.

—Anchorage Daily Times, *October 21, 1929*

"Have you ever been scared?" his father asks, staring off into the distance, trying not to sound too eager for an answer.

They sit on the back porch, drinking beer and eating plates of barbecue. They are having a party because Sam is home. Like every other party his parents have ever thrown, it fills the backyard and kitchen to overflowing. Already one of his cousins is drunk, with several more on the way to joining him. His mother's playing Elvis Presley's greatest hits, his Aunt Patty brought potato salad, and the next-door neighbor made chocolate cake. It is 1973 tonight, Sam thinks, and I am five years old, running around out there on the grass, staying up late because everyone is having too much fun to notice me. And he looks because he can't help it; he looks for himself with no idea what he would say to that little boy if he found him.

Has he ever been scared? There was the occasional fight in junior high and the time he nearly crashed his first car. He remembers his first kiss, his first touch, his first time. When has he not been scared? Scared of falling, of failing, of finding himself to be lacking. He has always been scared. But that is not what his father wants to know.

"No," he says, his voice strong and sure. "You can't be scared up there, you have to be confident. Fear will crash you; it will kill you. If I'm scared of flying then I shouldn't fly."

And this then is why Sam Beach has come home. Because at fifty feet looking for the runway in Barrow, you cannot notice for the first time that your plane is nearly out of fuel. You cannot realize at that moment, when the snow is blowing everywhere and the ground is gone, completely gone, that your fuel has vanished into all those delays, into flying heavy out of Kaktovik, into dragging all the way to Canada, into all those slow moments the way back of straying and forgetting and not paying attention. You cannot have your sudden moment of clarity then. You needed it thirty minutes or an hour ago. You needed it before you left that afternoon for Kaktovik, when you were already exhausted from flying half the day, when you were already making mistakes. You needed it two months ago when the Bosses told you to work more hours to "justify your paycheck." You needed it last year when they told you Barrow was only for six months, and you already knew they were liars. You needed it when it could have saved you, not now, when there is only silence and gravity and prayer.

Where is the runway, you ask yourself, where oh where is the runway?

And you talk to the airplane. You call her sweet and good and strong. You promise her an overhaul, a polishing, a total refurbishment. You promise to love her forever. And you look out that window and you lie on the radio. You say you see it, you say the runway is there because how can you admit that you are in trouble? And how would it help anyway if someone down there knew? All the time your palms are sweating, your shoulders cramping, and your hands, your stupid shaking hands, are gripping the yoke so tightly that the calluses crack and bleed.

And still you cannot see the runway.

Wait for it, wait and wait and wait. It is there, down there, it has to be there. And if you could reach down and grab it yourself you would, because you are trying that hard to see it, that hard to find it. And your whole life becomes that single stupid moment flying over the tundra looking for pavement in the middle of snow, looking for home.

Your whole life is that moment all alone at the top of the world where there is no one to look for you, no one to miss you, no one who loves you at all.

On his parents' porch, Sam doesn't realize that his hands have started shaking, that the beer is spilling slowly, gently, onto the concrete floor. His father reaches over and grabs hold of them, his own hands wet and smeared with sauce. His father holds his hands on the patio, while Elvis sings and all the pretty girls drift barefoot across the grass in dresses soft as spring. Sam thinks how he wants to bury his head in their hair, smelling lemonade and fireworks. He doesn't want to remember that last fifty feet, doesn't want to wake up anymore with desperate prayers, revisiting his dreams. He just wants that comfort found in the nape of a tanned neck, in a perfumed collarbone. He wants that bit of home found in a shoulder's sweet curve. He wants to see that five-year-old child again and tell that little boy not to go. This is the wrong adventure; this one is not yours. It will hurt you; it will break you.

He doesn't realize that his father hasn't asked the question again or that from across the yard his mother sees the two of them and has silently started to cry.

"It was the wrong flight," he tells his father, "the wrong flight on the wrong day."

And because he will never know, he will never understand, his father says nothing but listens to what Sam has to say. He listens for the stories he always knew his son needed to tell, the ones they have all been waiting to hear.

Sam has come home, and he knows why now.

Mrs. Thyra Merrill, wife of R. H. Merrill, the Anchorage flier who has been missing since last September, passed through Juneau on the steamer Admiral Tonys *last night, on her way to visit her parents, Mr. and Mrs. H. O. Allen Tigard of Portland, Oregon. Mrs. Merrill's two little boys accompanied her.*

Diligent search by air and water has failed to reveal the slightest clue and the disappearance of aviator Merrill remains one of the mysteries of air navigation in Alaska.

—The Daily Alaska Empire, *January 31, 1930*

20
Sam's Story

Years later we were sitting in the living room after a nice lunch with his parents when Sam started talking about Alaska. It was one of those conversations that none of us had enough anymore, and we jumped back into remembering the way it was, like all the stories were brand-new again. There was a guest there, a neighbor who walked by one day when Sam's father was outside mowing the lawn, and in the middle of a conversation about the weather and grass, he said that he used to work in Alaska and now was flying with a major airline. Sam's father invited him over and there we were, people who knew firsthand what aviation was like in Alaska. We were telling stories and we didn't think; we forgot who was listening.

We forgot that Sam's parents had never heard these stories.

Whenever he had told them something before, he always made sure it was about some other guy; some pilot he barely knew or hadn't met. It was always just a story he heard, something that might not even be completely true. "Pilots exaggerate a lot," he told them. "You never can tell the truth from a lie."

They liked knowing those stories, and because Sam told them so, they believed they were mostly not true. They heard about the bad weather and the crappy airplanes and all the almost crashes, and they laughed when Sam made it seem funny and thought they were inside a joke with him. They thought they knew something that others were missing, that others would probably never know.

———•———

We sat in their house after chicken salad and iced tea and talked with the neighbor who used to fly for the competition in Bethel. He wasn't out there that long, he said. He didn't have years in the North, but he had Bethel and that was enough. He had plenty of stories to share from Bethel.

So we talked about thousands of pounds of mail arriving all at once and not having enough time to move it. We talked about the competition always breathing down your neck, the postal inspector peeking in your windows, and the passengers calling from the village screaming about their late box or missing letter. We talked about the wind and the cold and snowdrifts from October to May. We talked about forty and fifty and sixty below and the skin on your hands cracking and your lips bleeding and using duct tape to fix your ski pants. And we didn't notice that Sam's parents weren't talking, and they weren't laughing anymore either.

We talked about Luke's crash into the mountain out-side Kotzebue and Joe Robinson hitting the mountain near Bettles on the way back from Anaktuvuk. We talked about Hageland's crashes and Yute's and all of Grant's near misses until they took five passengers down in 1999 and those poor guys stuck on that Northern Air Cargo flight that no one could save. We talked about hauling sled dogs and dead moose and buckets of salmon roe, but every story came back around to someone crashing, and then the guys started talk-ing about all of the times they almost crashed.

"How insane is it to be flying the pattern with no clue where all the traffic is around you because you can't see a damn thing?" says the neighbor. "If I told the guys I flew with now what flying weather in Bethel was like, they'd shit their pants." And we all laughed; we all enjoyed the joke of how it was and how no one could ever seem to believe it.

And Sam was so caught up in memories that he didn't see the way his mother kept wiping the coffee table even though the drinks were all on coasters or how his father was sitting as far back in his chair as he could and crossing his legs again and again, changing one over the other, stretching a knee, gripping an ankle.

The two of them kept shifting in careful little move-ments, tight movements, perfect movements. They kept moving like they thought they could get away, only they were living here and Sam was their son, and how far away could they go without leaving him behind?

I saw them out of the corner of my eye, watched them for a couple of minutes to see if maybe it was just me being paranoid, just me looking for a problem when there wasn't any, but it was there, it was real. This was them finally seeing how it really was for Sam, finally knowing that the only lies were the ones where he said he was okay; where he said those stories were never about him.

"Fly safe," they always told him. "Take care of yourself." And how could he let them think otherwise? How could he let them worry? And what could they do about it anyway?

"It's just a job," he always said to them, "I'm pretty good at it." And they asked him to send more pictures, more of the mountains and all that snow. They showed them to all their friends and said, "Isn't this pretty? Have you ever seen anything so pretty?" And Sam's funny stories were passed on, and people laughed and thought they knew all about flying in Alaska. They thought they knew what was happening to Sam Beach in places they had never heard of and circumstances they could not begin to understand.

And then we came and ate their food and sat on their couches, and the stories weren't so funny when we told them, even though we were laughing. They didn't sound funny at all to Sam's parents.

Quietly, so quietly, there in front of us they started to fall apart. The truth hurts sometimes, you know, when you finally, painfully, realize that what you're getting you can't deny. Sam's parents smiled graciously as we sat and talked, but they were breaking as we told our stories; like the thinnest wine glasses in a sink full of plates, they just broke. Maybe lies are a good thing, I thought watching them, maybe sometimes they are the right thing, the only thing. And were we more selfish for wanting to say how it really was, for needing to say it? Or were they the selfish ones for never wanting to hear any of it, for believing the most transparent lies in the world?

Flying in Alaska isn't hard? Who could honestly believe that; who would ever choose to believe something so obviously not true?

Sam's mom wipes the table again, and his dad gets up to bring more drinks even though our glasses are still full. And Sam must know; he has to know, but he doesn't stop talking. The stories are unstoppable this afternoon; they are overwhelming him and us, and we are happy to be full of them. We are happy not to have to lie yet again.

And the people who love Sam are just going to have to learn to live with that.

21

Reckoning

In 2007, ten years after I walked out the door, I went back.

The Company was still standing but empty. The hangar was there, the shed, the freezer; the buildings looked just like they always did, but the business was now over. No one was flying out of there anymore; that was clear to anyone who walked by. A hundred years might have gone by since the last time we were there. A blur from yesterday passed by me as I stood on the ramp of all those passengers and cargo, pilots, and planes I knew. It was forever ago in aviation years, and yet I could remember it like yesterday and I could see it perfectly; I could see *us*.

And for no good reason at all, I wished I was back there again.

It wasn't supposed to be like this. I came back to jog my memory, to take a few pictures so I could make sure I got the details right. But it was like seeing the house you grew up in or your old elementary school, that beach where you caught your first wave. Going back puts you into a different place, sends you through years you thought you had said goodbye to forever. It makes you remember more than you expect.

In 1997 we were all together; we were all on the job. There were the barbecues and the deck at Pike's and the bar at the Pumphouse. Bryce was still alive in 1997, and no one was struggling to understand how or why he died. It was a good summer; we just didn't realize how good. I didn't realize how good.

My father was still alive in 1997.

He never came to Alaska. I can't drive around Fairbanks and see places that he knew. But when I was with the Company still—when I was walking the ramp, banging out manifests on the old metal desk, running back and forth between Ops and the hangar—almost four thousand miles away my father was still alive. In this place at that time he is still back home working in his garden and listening to the Red Sox. As long as I was here, he is still there.

Here's one story: Twelve years ago my father died.

I have another story. Twelve years ago my brother and I were in our father's house, trying to decide what to keep and what should go. Our father was still alive; we started sorting through his things when he was dying. We were being practical. He knew about it, he understood it; everyone said it made sense. It was what we had to do; there was no real choice. We had to be practical, even while we were watching him die.

So why do I still have dreams about it? I dream that my father found a miracle and got better and came home and everything he owned was gone. His whole house was empty, given away and sold. Because we were practical.

The thing is, this is not a nightmare; it's a good dream, a happy dream. Because he got better; he came home.

It's my favorite dream.

———

In Alaska we got used to fast death. A guy you talked to in Kotzebue was gone the next day en route to Point Hope try-ing to move the mail in crap weather. A pilot flying a couple of buddies into Nulato crashed on a tight turn and went into the river. You flew into Barrow, picked up your load, and left while behind you the competition was crashing on takeoff. It always happened like that: A passenger we flew all the time cracked up on a snow machine; an employee fell into a bonfire in Galena; we had to fly the state troopers out to investigate a murder that happened two minutes after our scheduled flight left the village. It was a ten-second spot on the TV, a paragraph in the newspaper, or it wasn't even mentioned at all and we heard from someone who heard it from someone else. We all got used to high-speed loss, to moving on without slowing down.

But then there was this.

My friend John Hitz bought a brand-new red pickup after he'd been with the Company a couple of years. It was his first new car, and he loved that thing. He named it Red

Roy and treated it like a sports car. It was the biggest thing in his life, and he couldn't show it off enough.

I took my dog Jake to the vet one afternoon and my piece of crap thirty-year-old truck was dead in the parking lot when we came out. John lived the closest, so I called him to pick us up. He came right over but said Jake had to ride in the back—no dog fur on his new interior. It was cold outside, around twenty or so above, and Jake was not happy; but he jumped in the bed and we got inside, and because he had a soft heart, John opened up the back cab window so Jake could put his head in. And then when we were driving down the road in the snow, he called the dog to the window. And that's when Jake came through.

God, can you imagine it? We're driving at like forty miles per hour and we can hardly see in the snow and there's seventy-five pounds of German shepherd and husky and whatever the hell else Jake was coming in through the back window. John was screaming about his upholstery, and I knew there was no way that dog was going to be stopped. So I just started laughing; and the whole thing was hysterical and it ended up with Jake on my lap, John veering across two lanes of traffic, and fur everywhere.

There would have been a lot less fur if he had just let Jake up front in the first place.

So the only dog to ever ride in John Hitz's truck was my dog Jake. And I know that's true because one month later John was dead, hit by a truck while he was crossing the road on his snow machine. A stupid accident; a road accident. I bought John's truck from his parents and drove Jake everywhere in it, even cross-country when I went Outside. Jake is gone now, and God do I miss that dog, but I still have John's truck and I have that story. I'm the only one left to know it.

Everyone says it's silly to hold on to the truck. And I know it's more sentiment than anything else, but I don't care. It has over 120,000 miles and it's rusting. Someone hit me in Florida, and the rear bumper is banged up. The windshield is cracked from the Alaska Highway, and the headliner split in the cold. But it still runs great, even though it's scratched and faded and worn down. I don't feel too bad when one of my dogs gets fur in the cab anymore. But sometimes when I walk out in a parking lot and I'm just standing there, looking for my truck, I see it and the memories overwhelm me. I see it and for a second I think of John. I think I will turn around and see him again, that he will be here in a second to crack a joke about Scott or Tony or the Company. And then I grow up and I remember it's all gone. I know the truck is mine, that it has been mine far longer than John ever intended to make it his. And I know John is dead. But for a second sometimes I have him back, and that makes it worth it. Every time I remember him again, it's worth keeping that truck a little longer.

He was my friend. I should be allowed to do something foolish to remember my friend.

But who wants to hear that story? The part about Jake and the truck is good; it's always good. And everyone who knew John knew exactly how he would react to a dog climbing in his back window. John was the type to freak out when large furry creatures suddenly appeared. So that is a funny story; it is a laugh-out-loud story, and everybody loves it. But then someone asks, "Who is this guy? How come I never met him?"

And then I have to tell them about the snow machine and the crash and how one of the guys drove out there that night, hours later, and walked across the highway back and forth looking for pieces of John's sno-go, looking for anything that was left. Just little bits of metal and plastic on the side of the road—the stuff the troopers had swept out of the way. There was nothing else to collect, nothing else to save. And John was all the way dead and gone by then, dead and gone.

He was twenty-eight years old when he died, and now I'm past forty. I'm married; I have a son and a mortgage. And John is stuck in a picture on my bulletin board, smiling down at me from the wing of a Cessna 207 on Liberator Lake.

It's 1990 or 1991 and there's just flight time and snow and that girl he met who went back to England and maybe he loves her; he's not sure, but maybe.

It's 1992 and there are no dents or rust in his brand-new truck. We're at the Company Christmas party and John is drinking too much and the new parts girl is flirting with him and he's terrified of her. He's made a plan with the English girl and she's coming to visit; they're going to decide just what they should do.

It's not January 1993; it's not the funeral home. It's not John we've come to say good-bye to, all of us still on the young side of thirty. It's not John whose ashes were spread over Big Rock on Beaver Creek.

It's not John.

It wasn't John then or Luke or Bryce later. It was never anyone I knew in the stories I told; it was never anyone I knew.

And then my father died and there was no way to make up a name and pretend it was someone else. No hope to ever forget about that, no hope in hell of ever forgetting.

———•———

In the end, in those last weeks, my father lost his words. Out of frustration we played a game of pictures. We found stacks of them in his house, old photos, black-and-whites we had never seen before. I could find my father in the front row of Holy Family School, grinning with all the other kindergartners. He was a Boy Scout, a football player with the Catholic Youth Organization. He's posing with a model airplane. But there were so many others we did not know, boys in a street game of baseball; who were they? *Where* were they? Teenagers camping out with tents, making faces. Were these his friends? And then later, there's a beautiful woman waving at the camera, at my father holding the camera. We asked him who she was. "Pretty," he said, smiling.

"Was this picture from overseas?" we asked.

He nodded.

"In Spain?"

He nodded.

"Before you met Mom?"

"Yes."

"Who was she?"

And he thought about it. He tried. And then he said all he had: "Pretty," and reached for the picture. But he remembered her name for himself; I'm sure he knew her.

So we have a half dozen photos of a beautiful woman, my father's arm around her, the two of them laughing, their heads thrown back. They were so happy together. We always thought our mother was his first serious girlfriend, and now we have to wonder. Was this girl his true love, his real happily ever after? Was this the girl he should have married?

Would it have made a difference?

———•———

Bryce Donovan went into the Yukon River the same week my father died. I was choosing pictures to display at the funeral, trying to score a balance between each period of his life. I was not a child in those hours, I was an archaeologist; I was the curator of my father's memorial museum.

Bryce died when I was deep in my own childhood, considering the sentimental value of a day at the beach versus a backyard sandbox. Which was more authentic, which showed him best as the father I remembered?

And what pictures were Bryce's kids going to choose for their father's funeral?

———•———

It was the oddest thing, being back on that ramp after so many years. After I left it wasn't my place anymore, my territory. I wasn't the one at the center of the storm. Now, though, there was no storm. There was just the wreckage of an airline that no longer flew and the broken planes that used to serve it.

The few aircraft still parked on the ramp looked like they had been dumped. Most of them I had never seen before, except for 86C, propped up on crates and missing its engine cowling. The front wheel was gone and somewhere along the line the door was removed and replaced with a mismatched piece that didn't fit. From the sturdy little Piper Saratoga we used to fly up north several days a week, now it was on life support; good for parts and little else.

Just like the rest of the Company.

Nobody was flying around me that evening; there was a fire burning close to Town and the smoke made flight-seeing impossible. It was quiet enough to hear the voices I wanted to hear; the memory voices. Shawn or Bill pulling 86C up so we could get it loaded and ready to go; one of the Navajos parked behind it for the afternoon flight, the passengers standing around talking on the front porch.

There really was nothing left here, not for me, not for any of us. But I wanted there to be.

The Company was the hardest job I ever had, and I should have been glad to leave it behind; I should have felt nothing but relief. But after all the noise of the job was gone, I found myself left with a lot of silence, an enormous deafening silence. And it scared me; it scared away everything I thought I was. Because the Company kept on going even after I left. Just like the owners had always said about everyone else, I learned I was replaceable too. I had no right to be surprised;

I should have known by then that replacement was the only consistent thing about Alaska aviation—that once you're gone, everyone forgets you were ever there. But still, it hurt.

There was no victory being the one taking pictures after the place had gone out of business. By then winning didn't matter anymore; nothing like winning and losing mattered at all. It was just me and my camera and all those years of who I was and who I cared about and who we were. It was just us again, working for the Company. It was just us and everything we knew about flying in a place that lives only in our stories now and a time that will always stand still.

I can see us when I close my eyes; I can see us all. And I'm not sorry for that. I'm not sorry for wanting to see that place and time like it was; some memories we just don't want to ever let go.

———•———

A couple of years ago for Christmas I bought my brother the *Star Wars* trilogy on DVD. I wrote in the card how one of my favorite memories was back in 1977, when *Star Wars* was first released and Daddy drove us thirty minutes out of town to a theater that was showing the movie on opening night. Afterwards, while my brother and I were shocked and stunned and completely in love with everything we had seen, our father laughed at us and said it was silly; it was just like the Saturday serials he used to watch when he was a kid, before the *real* movie came on. But even when he laughed he was enjoying it with us; he was smiling with us. We were all a part of that moment.

I love that memory.

Christmas morning my brother called to thank me and then said that he didn't remember that, didn't remember any of it. He remembered the movie but not where he saw it or who he was with. All of that was forgotten. And I realized that now there are only the things that I remember and the things he remembers that are left. And everything else is what we don't even know to look for anymore, what we don't even know we are missing. And if we don't keep all of it together somehow, then someday there might be nothing. There will just be pictures of a boy playing football, a man holding my hand, and the three of us catching waves. And I will tell my son that this was my father; that I loved him but he died a long time ago. And my son will put the pictures aside because that won't be enough; a face on a page won't be enough for him.

My father will just be someone who is dead that he never knew, someone who doesn't mean anything to him at all.

———•———

I'm forty-two years old now and I'm forgetting. And maybe, really, that is the only reason I wrote this. Because when Scott and I talk he tells me that he doesn't remember either, that he still knows the names or at least the faces, but he is forgetting who they really were, how some of them died, and why. Worst of all, he is forgetting who we were back then, who we were before. And Sam isn't telling his stories at all anymore, because everyone he works with keeps calling him a liar. It couldn't be that cold, couldn't blow that hard. He couldn't know that many dead pilots. And he doesn't want to fight about it so he just says nothing. He says Alaska is just like the nature shows and books say it is. He says there's a lot of snow. And then he says a lot of nothing.

———•———

Stories are funny because they won't let you ignore them; they demand to be written. And maybe you think if you put them down, if you let them leave your head and put them on paper, then they will live forever. Maybe you can even cheat death that way.

Or maybe I'm just wondering if anybody still listens and wants to know who we were. Maybe I want to know if stories still matter or if the truth really can disappear with the dead and leave you standing there without any chance of ever knowing what really happened. No chance in hell of knowing anything at all.

You think you had a whole history, a past that was tied to a place and a time, and yet when you go back there it's all gone, vanished. You stand in the same place where you stood so many times before and there is nothing left, no hint at all of what you did, of who you were, of what mattered so much to you and all your friends.

We were wiped away, just like Eielson's company, and Merrill's and Wien's. Once upon a time we were something; we made things happen. And now you would never know our names. Even if you drove by the Company right now, this very minute, you would never know my name. But I was here once; we all were. For a time that didn't last nearly long enough, all of us were here. And I remember. Sam and Tony and Frank and Scott and Bob and Casey and Bryce. All those years before, I remember, I remember.

February 23, 1999

Dear Colleen,
Here's the reports that I got on the 22nd. As I get other news, I'll pass it on to you. Right now I'm alright. I kind of expected the news that I got but I did not expect the short time. There's not a lot to say now, nor a lot that can be done.
Please take care of yourself and be careful.
Love,
Dad

I promise. Forever, I'll remember.

Acknowledgments

First and foremost, deep appreciation to Jessa Crispin and Michael Schaub at Bookslut.com, and Tom Dooley at Eclectica.org, who gave me my first gigs reviewing books and thus ushered my entry into publishing. I still write for all of them and continue to be grateful for their support. A special shout out to author Bennett Madison, who wrote about a delightful girl detective named Lulu Dark whose adventures I reviewed in 2005, and thus became acquainted with his agent, Rebecca Sherman of Writers House. When I had a completed manuscript for *The Map Of My Dead Pilots* prepared, Rebecca was one of the people from whom I sought advice. She not only offered her support but passed along some pages to her colleague Michele Rubin, who shortly became my agent and made this book happen in more ways than I can list. Through Michele's dedication and diligence, *Map* made its way to Lyons Press and Holly Rubino, who has been a thoughtful and wise editor each step of the way.

I can never express enough what Michele has meant to my success, and I remain grateful for how much she continues to believe in me.

Before *Map* existed there were people who said the right thing at the right time—from Johnny Williams, who dreamed of writing books with me back when we were both terrifically young to Dave German, who sat beside me in 078 on the ramp in Fairbanks during a very, very bad day. There has also been a small group of dear friends, book lovers all, who supported my every effort through e-mails from across the country and around the world—you know who you are and how much your encouragement has meant; I couldn't have done it without you. And Mom, well, you know don't you? You always knew.

For Ward and Pierce, there are no words to say other than you fill my heart, both of you, each and every day. And for Patrick Mondor, the best brother ever, there are a thousand memories that belong now only to you and me. I could not have made it through every moment without you. As always, you remain forever my hero.

Finally, when I first started writing about the Company, it was long after dark with my dogs Jake and Tucker at my feet. As I type these words, it is with their successors, Hondo and Indy, sprawled out nearby. Many writers have told stories of late nights alone with their words; I am glad to have had with me the best of companions as I put mine together.

About the Author

Colleen Mondor is a longtime columnist for *Bookslut* and book reviewer for *Booklist* whose essays have appeared in several journals and aviation publications. She learned to fly at eighteen and spent four years running Operations for a bush commuter in Fairbanks, Alaska. She lives in the Pacific Northwest and Alaska, and her website can be found at www.chasingray.com.